PAULA DEEN'S
my first cookbook

Paula Deen

with Martha Nesbit
Illustrated by Susan Mitchell

SIMON & SCHUSTER BOOKS FOR YOUNG READERS

NEW YORK · LONDON · TORONTO · SYDNEY

This book is for
the love of my life,
my grandson
Jack Linton Deen,
in hopes that he, too,
will inherit the love
of the kitchen.

SIMON & SCHUSTER BOOKS FOR YOUNG READERS · An imprint of Simon & Schuster Children's Publishing Division · 1230 Avenue of the Americas, New York, New York 10020 · Copyright © 2008 by Paula Deen · All rights reserved, including the right of reproduction in whole or in part in any form. · SIMON & SCHUSTER BOOKS FOR YOUNG READERS is a trademark of Simon & Schuster, Inc. · Book design by Alicia Mikles · The text for this book is set in McKracken. · The illustrations for this book are rendered in watercolor. · Manufactured in China · 10 9 8 7 6 5 4 3 2 1 · Library of Congress Cataloging-in-Publication Data · Deen, Paula H, 1947– · Paula Deen's my first cookbook / by Paula Deen with Martha Nesbit : Illustrated by Susan Mitchell. · p. cm. – (Simon & Schuster books for young readers) · ISBN-13: 978-1-4169-5033-2 · ISBN-10: 1-4169-5033-8 · 1. Cookery–Juvenile literature. I. Nesbit, Martha Giddens. II. Mitchell, Susan. III. Title. · TX652.5.D44 2008 · 641.5'123–dc22 · 2008004433

first
edition

Acknowledgments

I would like to acknowledge every one of the children in my past who have inspired me to want to do this cookbook for them. How happy I am to see you discovering your kitchens. And, of course, I acknowledge Maggie Shehane and Marlie Stineman, who tested many of the recipes in Savannah, Georgia, with my collaborator, Martha Nesbit.

In New York, I'd like to thank Emily Meehan, senior editor; Courtney Bongiolatti, assistant editor; Dorothy Gribbin, managing editor; Lizzy Bromley and Alicia Mikles, designers; Susan Mitchell, illustrator; and Suzanne Fass, copy editor.

As always, my work would be impossible without the professional support of the Paula Deen Team.

Finally, I'd like to acknowledge Jamie and Brooke Dean for giving me and our family Jack.

This cookbook is for my littlest fans.

I had no idea when I started cooking on television that some of my biggest admirers would be tiny tots! But everywhere I go, mamas and daddies, grandmothers and grandfathers, aunts and uncles tell me that their children are glued to the tube when I'm on the air. Thank you for that!

So, several years back, I started dreaming about a special cookbook for the youngest cooks. Why? Well, because food has played such an important part in my life, and I believe it can play an important part in your lives, too. Every dish that I make brings back a memory that can't be taken away. It might remind me of my grandmother Paul, or my grandmother Hiers, or Aunt Peggy, or Aunt Trina, or of Jamie, or Bobby, or Bubba, or Michael, or some wonderful cook who shared a recipe or a special event with me.

I wrote this cookbook just for you because cooking is a creative outlet, like painting or dancing. Passing along the art of cooking will empower you, and remind you that you can do anything you set your mind to.

So, rattle those pots and pans, my little angels, and get to creating those memories!

With love, from my kitchen to yours,

Paula Deen
Savannah, Georgia
October 2008

A Message to Adults
Who Are Cooking with Kids

I would like to thank Maggie Shehane, an eight-year-old in the third grade at Savannah Country Day School, and Marlie Stineman, a seven-year-old in the second grade at Richmond Hill Elementary, who tested many of my recipes. They taught me a lot about cooking with kids. Here's what you should know:

Maggie and Marlie quickly developed skills from one session to the next. In the beginning they could barely break an egg, but in no time they were cracking eggs like pros. Their favorite tasks: setting the timer, stirring, cracking eggs, making turnovers, and using the mixer.

In the process of learning to cook, Maggie and Marlie tried many foods that they had never tried before. Their parents and grandparents reported that they had become more adventuresome eaters at home as well.

Once they became familiar with a few culinary techniques, they began to experiment with recipes at home. Both of them have made breakfast several times. Marlie has created several tinfoil-baked items (carrots and potatoes and chicken) after learning how to make Campfire Stew (see page 76).

Cooking can be very dangerous for young children. Therefore I recommend that you supervise them at all times. I recommend that you use the sharp knife if it's called for in a recipe, as elementary-age children can get very distracted and look up from the cutting board, with disastrous results. Also, watch out for burns—kids have a tendency to rest their arms on the pot rim while stirring at the cooktop. I also had some near burns of hands and arms that got too close to hot pans that had just come from the oven.

Cooking with young children is FUN for them and even more fun for you. My mission was to excite a new generation of cooks, and I believe this cookbook will do just that.

Jamie, age 2, and me

Contents

Safety First!

Cooking can be dangerous! I'm serious!
Just like any other fun activity, like riding your bicycle or playing soccer,
there are special safety gear and rules for the kitchen.

- **MOST IMPORTANT:** Remember, what you can do on your own depends on how old you are, so always check with your adult helper before doing anything in the kitchen by yourself!

- Only cook when an adult is there to help you, especially if you are cutting, opening cans, boiling, frying, or taking something out of the oven. If your adult helper says it's okay, you can make a few of these recipes without help, like Ants on a Log (page 101).

- If your adult helper says it's okay to use a knife, always use a cutting board when cutting. When using a knife or vegetable parer, always cut away from yourself.

- Wash your hands a lot. There are germs on just about everything— the food you are using, your hands, the countertops, and the cutting board. Wash your hands after handling any food, and before putting anything in your mouth, like cookie dough.

- Wear an apron, smock, or shirt that you don't mind getting dirty when you cook. Don't cook in long sleeves. They can get caught on the pots and pans, can drag through your food, or, if you get too close to the heat on the stove, they can catch on fire.

- Have hot pads or oven mitts handy. If your adult helper says you're old enough to use the stovetop, you can use hot pads or oven mitts any time you are taking a pan out of the oven or taking a lid off of a pot. Otherwise your adult helper should take care of those tasks for you.

- Use a step stool so that you are comfortable at the counter or in front of the cooktop. Don't try to cut or cook standing on your tippy toes.
- Turn pot handles to the back of the cooktop, away from the heat of any burners, so that you don't accidentally knock a pot or pan over on yourself!
- Wear closed-toe shoes to protect your piggies from a dropped can or broken glass.
- Turn off the heat when you take a pan or pot off the cooktop. Turn off the oven when you've finished cooking.
- Rinse fruits, vegetables, chicken, fish, and meat under cold water before you eat or cook them. Pat dry. This will rinse away most of the bacteria.

Two More Things . . .

- If you want your adult helper to want to cook with you more than once, you'd better clean up after yourself. Put warm, soapy water in the sink and wash and rinse each dish you use. Let the dishes air-dry on the drainboard, which helps cut down on germs. Or put them in the dishwasher if your family has one. An adult will probably have to help you put the dishes away.
- If you want to be a successful kid chef, use a trick all the real chefs use: Get out everything you will need to make a recipe—the utensils and the ingredients. That makes things go smoother when you are actually cooking.

Glossary

Everything worth doing has its own special vocabulary—fishing, skiing, and playing hopscotch, my personal favorite! Well, cooking has a vocabulary, too. Here are some words you will learn when you cook:

 BAKE - Cook in the oven. There are top and bottom burners, and the heat from baking comes from the ones in the bottom of the oven.

 BEAT - Mix two or more ingredients with a spoon or a mixer until they are smooth.

 BOIL - Cook on top of the cooktop in a pot until you see bubbles. The hotter the temperature, the bigger the bubbles.

 BROIL - Cook in a very hot oven until the top gets brown and bubbly. The heat for broiling comes from the burners in the top of the oven. You usually leave the oven door cracked open a little when you broil.

 CHOP - Cut food into pieces with a knife. The recipe will tell you if the pieces should be big or small.

 CUBE - Cut food into little squares all the same size.

 DICE - Cut food into teeny pieces all the same size.

FLOUR – This is a white powdery ingredient that you use to make cookies, cakes, and bread. Sometimes, a recipe will tell you to "flour" a pan, which means that you will put about a tablespoon of flour into a buttered pan and shake the pan until the flour coats all the sides and the bottom of the pan.

FOLD – This is stirring really gently (the opposite of "beat") with a rubber spatula, going deep into the batter and lifting it over on top of itself, like how you might fold up your dinner napkin.

GARNISH – Edible decoration that you put on a plate before you serve whatever it is you cooked—a little sprig of parsley, a slice of lemon, a berry, or a cherry tomato, for example.

GRATE – Rub food against a grater to make slivers. Watch your fingers and fingernails!

GREASE – This is like flour—it's a noun *and* a verb! *Grease,* the noun, is a fat, like butter or shortening or bacon grease. When the directions tell you to "grease" the pan, you rub the fat over the inside surface of the pan.

KNEAD – This is a fun activity where you take dough and slap it on your countertop, press into it with both palms, then fold the top over the bottom and turn the dough. Do it again and again and again! Sometimes (usually) you have to add a little flour to the dough to keep it from sticking.

 **MELT** - Heat something solid, like butter, until it becomes a liquid.

 MINCE - This is like "dice," only smaller—cut food into tiny pieces that are the same size.

 **PAN-FRY** - This is cooking food on top of the cooktop in a skillet in a little oil or butter.

 PARE - Cut off the skin of a potato or apple.

 PEEL - Pull off the skin of a banana or orange or onion, or the shell from a hard-cooked egg.

 **ROLL OUT** - Flatten with a rolling pin or your fingertips— usually biscuits, cookies, bread or pizza dough.

 **SAUTÉ** - This is almost the same as "pan-fry." Cook in a skillet on the cooktop in a small amount of fat. The difference is that when you pan-fry, you usually don't turn the food but once or twice. When you sauté, you keep turning it over and over until all the food gets done.

 SCRAPE DOWN - When mixing food, take a rubber spatula and push down all of the food on the sides of the bowl so that it gets mixed in good.

SIFT - Put dry ingredients in a sifter and turn the handle until all of the stuff (like flour) gets mixed up and comes out of the holes in the bottom.

SIMMER - Cook in a pot on the cooktop over low heat until there are tiny bubbles all around the sides of the food in the pot.

SPRINKLE - Take one ingredient and scatter it lightly over the top of something else.

STIR - Mix with a spoon.

TOSS - Don't throw it! Mix it very lightly.

WHIP - Use a mixer to beat something vigorously, like cream or egg whites. This is super fun!

WHISK - Another noun-and-verb word! A whisk is an instrument that looks like the beaters on an electric mixer. You use it to mix things like eggs and to stir sauces so they will be smooth. When a recipe says to "whisk" something, you use a whisk to stir the ingredients together.

How to Measure

Measuring is important when you cook. You can't just guess—you have to use the exact amount that the recipe tells you to if you want your cookies and cupcakes to taste good.

DRY

LIQUID

There are two types of measuring cups: One type is used for dry ingredients, and the other is used for liquid ingredients. However, sometimes the "dry" ingredients aren't dry: You use a "dry" measuring cup to measure mayonnaise and sour cream.

Cup sizes

One-fourth ($^1/_4$)
One-third ($^1/_3$)
One-half ($^1/_2$)
One cup

To measure white sugar and flour

Dip the dry-type measuring cup into the flour and fill it until it is heaping full. Take the back of a butter knife and scrape off the top until it is level.

To measure brown sugar

Spoon the brown sugar into the measuring cup you use for dry ingredients and pat down until the sugar is even with the top of the cup. You do this just like you do wet sand in a bucket on the beach. When you turn the sugar out, it should be in the shape of the cup.

To measure butter

Butter has measuring marks on the wrapper so you can just cut off what you need.
One-fourth ($^1/_4$) stick equals two tablespoons
One-half ($^1/_2$) stick equals one-fourth ($^1/_4$) cup
Six tablespoons equals one-third ($^1/_3$) cup

One stick equals one-half ($^1/_2$) cup
Two sticks equal one cup

To measure cut-up foods

Cut them up first, then place them into the measuring cup you use for dry ingredients until they reach the top of the cup.

To measure liquids

Use a liquid measuring cup and put it on the counter. Stand so that your eyes are even with the cup. Pour in the water, juice, milk, or oil until it reaches the line exactly on the cup.

To measure salt

Stand by the sink and pour the salt into the measuring spoon. Level it with your fingertips.

To measure baking powder, baking soda, pepper, and cinnamon or other spices

Dip the measuring spoon into the container and get a heaping spoonful of whatever you are measuring. Press the spoon against the side of the container and pull out the spoon—the ingredient will be packed into the spoon. Or you can level off the ingredients with the back of a butter knife, or the side of your finger!

To measure liquids in a spoon

Pour them into the spoon over the sink or a bowl or cup until they reach the top. Have the bowl you are adding them to nearby so you won't have to walk with the liquid in the spoon.

How to Set a Table

🌼 Ask your adult helper to show you what you have to choose from, a tablecloth or placemats.

Whether you use a tablecloth or placemats, every setting includes:

🌼 A plate, set right in front of the person who is eating.

🌼 A knife to the right of the plate, with the blade of the knife facing in toward the plate.

🌼 A spoon to the right of the knife.

🌼 A fork to the left of the plate.

🌼 A napkin to the left of the fork, or underneath the fork. You can even learn to fold napkins and place these directly on the plate, like in a fancy restaurant.

🌼 The glass is always at the top of the knife, a little to the left.

🌼 If you are serving bread, you can place a small plate above the fork.

🌼 If you are serving salad, you can place a small bowl above the fork.

🌼 A centerpiece in the middle of the table can make your dinner special—a small vase with flowers or greenery from your yard, a candle in a pretty holder, a bowl of apples or lemons, or even a favorite keepsake from your room.

Good Manners

*Just like there are rules in the kitchen,
there are rules at the table when you are eating.*

♥ Wait until everyone has been seated before you pick up your fork
to eat. At our house, the eating doesn't begin until after we've said the
blessing.

♥ Put your napkin in your lap so that spills will get on your napkin, not
your clothes. Use your napkin to wipe your hands and your mouth.

♥ Don't chew with your mouth open—people can see the chewed-up food.

♥ Don't talk while you are chewing—people can see the chewed-up food.

♥ No elbows on the table.

♥ Cut big pieces of food into little pieces with your knife and fork. Get an
adult to show you how. Don't pick up a big piece of meat with your
fork and just bite off a piece.
Exception: Some foods it's okay to eat with your hands, like fried
shrimp and chicken. Just pick 'em up and bite 'em!

♥ If you need something, ask for it. Don't reach. Say, "Please pass the . . ."

♥ If you are having bread and you want butter, take your knife and get
some butter off of the butter dish and scrape it onto your bread plate
or dinner plate. Then butter your roll or bread from the butter on
your plate.

♥ When you have eaten all of your food, put your knife and fork together
across the top of your plate. This signals that you are all done!

♥ Compliment the cook. "That was a delicious meal, Mom (or Dad)."
Hopefully, if you are the cook, someone will compliment *you!*

♥ When everyone is done, ask if you may be excused. If you are,
take your dish to the trash can, scrape it, and place it in the sink or
dishwasher.

*These rules will make you a very special guest who is comfortable
eating in restaurants and in other people's homes.
There are lots more rules, but we'll just start with these for now.*

17

CHAPTER 1

Mornin',

Me in third or fourth grade at Baconton Elementary, in Georgia

Sunshine!

Pancakes

What you'll need

Dry measuring cups
(1 cup and 1/4 cup)

Cookie sheet,
for measuring

Large bowl

Liquid
measuring cup

Measuring spoons

Whisk

Rubber spatula

Drinking cup

Pastry brush

Nonstick skillet, electric
skillet, or griddle

Wide spatula

Big plate

2 cups baking mix

1 cup whole milk

1 teaspoon baking
powder

1 teaspoon sugar

2 eggs

A little oil in a
drinking cup

Butter

Syrup or jelly

20

What you'll do

1. Measure the baking mix with the 1-cup dry measuring cup over the cookie sheet and put the baking mix into the mixing bowl. Measure the milk with the liquid measuring cup and put it in the mixing bowl. Measure the baking powder and sugar with a measuring spoon and put them in the bowl. Crack the eggs one at a time by tapping them against the cookie sheet. Hold the cracked part of an egg in front of you over the bowl and, using your thumbs, push into the shell and pull apart the two sides. Throw out the shells. Using the whisk, stir the ingredients until they are mixed.

2. Scrape down the sides of the bowl with the rubber spatula. Mix the batter again with the spatula.

3. Dip the pastry brush into the oil and then brush it in the skillet or electric frying pan or on the griddle. You may need an adult to help you with this.

4. Heat the pan to medium-high. (A drop of water will dance around.) If you are using an electric skillet, turn the dial to 375 degrees.

5. Use the ¼ cup to dip out batter. Pour it into the skillet or onto the hot griddle.

6. Cook the pancakes until bubbles form all over the tops of the pancakes.

7. Flip each pancake with the wide spatula.

8. Pile the pancakes on a plate as they get done, golden brown on the bottom.

9. Serve hot with butter and syrup or jelly.

Makes about 12 pancakes

21

Bull's Eye
What you'll need

Biscuit cutter

Small nonstick
skillet

Wide spatula

Small plate

1 slice of whole-wheat
bread per person

2 thin pats of butter
per person

1 egg
per person

Salt and pepper

Hot sauce, if you like it

What you'll do

1. Cut a hole in the center of the bread with the biscuit cutter.

2. Put one pat of butter in the skillet and melt it over low heat. Have your adult helper nearby for this.

3. Put the bread on top of the melted butter. Tap the egg gently on the side of the counter and then pull the sides apart with your fingers, breaking it right over the hole in the bread. If you break the yolk, that's okay! Sprinkle a little bit of salt into the palm of your hand, then brush it onto the egg. Sprinkle a little bit of pepper into the palm of your hand, then brush a little bit onto the egg.

4. Let the egg cook until the bread is golden on the bottom, about 2 minutes.

5. Use the wide spatula to turn the bread, egg and all. While you have it lifted up, let your adult helper put the other pat of butter into the pan and when it is melted, turn the bread with the egg over on the other side. Cook the bull's eye until it looks like it is done, about 2 minutes more.

6. Use the wide spatula to remove the bull's eye to the plate.

7. Eat with a splash of hot sauce if you like it. I do—I like Texas Pete!

Serves 1

Green Eggs and Ham

Make this for your family on St. Patrick's Day!

What you'll need

Medium bowl

Whisk

Medium nonstick skillet

Wooden spoon

Wide spatula

2 small plates

3 eggs

Salt and pepper

1 drop of blue food coloring

1/4 cup minced ham

What you'll do

1. One by one, crack the eggs on the side of the counter. Break the eggs into the bowl by pushing gently into the crack with your thumbs and pulling the two sides of the shell apart. Throw out the shells. Add a pinch of salt and a pinch of pepper and one drop of blue food coloring (remember, blue and yellow make green!). Whisk the eggs until they are completely mixed together.

2. Heat the skillet until it is medium-hot. Making sure your adult helper is nearby, add the ham and cook it until it begins to brown a little, about 3 minutes. Stir it with the wooden spoon to keep it from sticking.

3. Pour the eggs in right on top of the ham. Don't stir until the eggs have begun to set, about 2 minutes. Take the spatula and fold the cooked eggs over. Chop up the eggs with the tip of the spatula. Do this a couple of times, until all of the egg is cooked.

4. Remove eggs to small plates as soon as they are done.

Serves 2

Cheese Eggs with Onions and Ham

What you'll need

Medium nonstick skillet

Wooden spoon

Medium bowl

Whisk

Wide spatula

2 small plates

2 tablespoons butter

¼ cup minced ham from deli slices or from a piece of center-cut ham

¼ cup minced onion

3 eggs

½ teaspoon salt and a sprinkling of pepper

½ cup grated sharp Cheddar cheese

What you'll do

1. Melt the butter in the skillet over low heat. Always have your adult helper nearby when you're at the stove. Add the minced ham and onion and cook this until the onion starts to get a little brown, about 10 minutes. Stir with the wooden spoon while they cook. Turn off the heat while you are cracking the eggs.

2. One by one, crack the eggs on the side of the counter. Break the eggs into the bowl by pushing gently into the crack with your thumbs and pulling the two sides of the shell apart. Throw out the shells. Add the salt to the eggs. Sprinkle the pepper into the palm of your hand and then brush it into the eggs. Whisk the eggs until they are all mixed up.

3. Turn the heat back on to medium-high and pour in the eggs on top of the ham and onion. Allow the eggs to cook until you see them starting to set.

4. Reduce the heat to low. With your spatula, fold the cooked eggs over the raw part so that the raw part gets to the bottom of the pan. Use the tip of the spatula to chop up the eggs in big pieces.

5. When you think the eggs are just about done, sprinkle the cheese evenly over the eggs. When you see it beginning to melt, use the spatula to chop it up into the eggs so it is evenly distributed.

6. Divide the eggs between the two plates and serve.

Serves 2

Mexican Omelets

What you'll need

Medium bowl

Whisk

Medium nonstick skillet

Wide spatula

Butter knife

2 small plates

3 eggs

1/2 teaspoon salt and a
sprinkling of pepper

2 tablespoons butter

1/4 cup grated
Monterey Jack cheese or
4-cheese Mexican blend

2 tablespoons
mild salsa

2 tablespoons
sour cream

What you'll do

1. One by one, crack the eggs by tapping each one on the side of the counter. Break the eggs into the bowl by pushing into the crack with your thumbs and pulling the two sides of the shell apart. Throw out the shells. Add the salt to the eggs. Sprinkle the pepper into the palm of your hand and then brush it into the eggs. Whisk the eggs until they are all mixed up.

2. Ask your adult helper to help you heat the skillet to medium-high heat and melt the butter. Pour the eggs on top of the melted butter and let them sit for about a minute, until you see the edges starting to set. Then take the spatula, run it along the inside edge of the pan, and lift up one edge of the omelet. Let your adult helper tilt the pan so that the raw egg can run underneath. Keep doing this until there is no raw egg left. The omelet will look like an egg pancake.

3. Remove the pan from the cooktop and sprinkle the cheese right down the middle of the omelet. Take the spatula and fold one side of the omelet over, almost to the other edge. Then fold over the other side. Use the knife to cut the omelet in half.

4. Take the pan over to your plates and, using the spatula, carefully slide one half of the omelet onto one plate, and the other half onto the other plate.

5. Top each omelet half with 1 tablespoon of salsa and 1 tablespoon of sour cream.

Serves 2

French Toast

What you'll need

Glass pie plate

Whisk

Medium nonstick skillet

Wide spatula

2 small plates

1 egg

⅛ teaspoon cinnamon

3 tablespoons sugar

1 tablespoon milk

2 slices of bread, white or whole-wheat

2 tablespoons butter

Toppings

Butter

Syrup or jelly

Peanut butter

What you'll do

1. Tap the egg on the side of the counter and then crack it into the pie plate by pushing in with your thumbs and pulling the shell apart. Throw out the shell. Add the cinnamon, sugar, and milk and whisk everything together. Put one piece of bread in the egg and flip it so that both sides get good and soggy.

2. With an adult helper nearby, heat the skillet over medium heat. Put both pieces of butter as far apart as you can in the skillet. Let the butter melt. Put the piece of soggy bread on top of the butter. Soak the second piece of bread and put it on top of the rest of the butter. Let the toast cook for about 1 minute, then use the spatula to flip the bread onto the other side. Let the second side cook about a minute, too.

3. Put each piece of toast on a plate. Spread with butter, syrup, jelly, or peanut butter.

Serves 2

Cheese Toast
What you'll need

Tray from the
toaster oven

Oven mitt or hot pad

Pizza cutter

2 plates

2 slices of bread, white
or whole-wheat

1/3 cup grated sharp
Cheddar cheese

1 thick slice of
Swiss cheese

What you'll do

1. Put the two pieces of bread side by side on the toaster oven tray. On one piece of bread, sprinkle on the Cheddar cheese evenly. Put the slice of Swiss cheese on the other piece of bread.

2. Put the tray in the toaster oven and set it to the longest toaster setting. Watch your toast cook through the window in the oven.

3. When it is bubbly, turn off the oven. Use the oven mitt or the hot pad to carefully remove the tray. An adult may have to help you. Use the pizza cutter to cut each piece of toast into two halves. You and a friend can each have a yellow piece of cheese toast and a white piece of cheese toast.

Serves 2

Cinnamon Rolls
What you'll need

Cookie sheet

Parchment paper

Oven mitts or hot pads

Plates and forks

1 can of refrigerated
crescent rolls (8 rolls)

8 large marshmallows

Cinnamon sugar, made by mixing $1/2$ cup
sugar with 1 teaspoon cinnamon

What you'll do

1. Turn on the oven to 375 degrees.

2. Separate the dough into 8 triangles. Place 1 marshmallow right in the middle of each triangle. Sprinkle each marshmallow with some of the cinnamon sugar.

3. Bring up all of the sides of the roll to completely cover the marshmallow, pinching all of the edges together so that none of the marshmallow shows.

4. Cover the cookie sheet with a piece of parchment paper. Place the rolls on the parchment paper, making sure none of them are touching. Sprinkle with more cinnamon sugar.

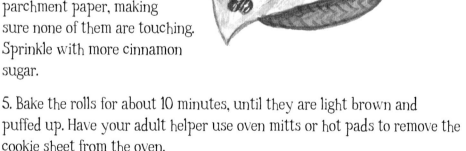

5. Bake the rolls for about 10 minutes, until they are light brown and puffed up. Have your adult helper use oven mitts or hot pads to remove the cookie sheet from the oven.

6. Serve warm on plates, with forks to eat them with.

Makes 8 cinnamon rolls

Fruit Kebabs
What you'll need

Wooden skewers

One 8-ounce can of
pineapple chunks, drained

1 pint ripe strawberries, rinsed,
patted dry, and stem ends cut off

Green grapes

Red grapes

What you'll do

Alternate pieces of pineapple, strawberries, and red and green grapes on the skewers. Be careful not to stick the skewers into your fingers when you are putting on the fruit. Do not put the sharp end of the skewer into your mouth. To eat, remove the fruit with your fingers.

Makes about a dozen small fruit skewers, depending on how much fruit you put on each one

Monkey Bread
What you'll need

Pie plate

Cutting board

Butter knife

Small pot

Wooden spoon

Bundt pan

Oven mitts or hot pads

Wire rack

Big cake plate

1 cup white sugar

2 teaspoons cinnamon

3 cans of refrigerator biscuits (10 biscuits each)

1 stick butter

1 cup brown sugar

Cooking spray

What you'll do

1. Turn on the oven to 325 degrees.

2. Put the white sugar and cinnamon in the pie plate and mix them together with your fingers until they are completely mixed. Remove the biscuits from the tubes. Place each biscuit on the cutting board and cut each one into fourths using the butter knife. Place each piece of biscuit into the cinnamon sugar and shake it all around until it is coated. (You can do a few at a time.)

3. With an adult helper nearby, put the butter and brown sugar into the pot and heat it over low heat until it is mixed together. Stir it with the wooden spoon. Turn off the heat.

4. Spray the Bundt pan with cooking spray. Place the biscuit pieces evenly in the Bundt pan. Pour the brown sugar mixture over the biscuits.

5. Bake the biscuits in the oven for 35 minutes. Have your adult helper use oven mitts or hot pads to remove the Bundt pan and place it on the wire rack to cool for 10 minutes.

6. To serve, turn the Bundt pan upside down onto the cake plate. The biscuits should fall right out. Let the monkey bread cool for a few minutes so that you don't burn your fingers or mouth. Pinch off pieces to eat.

Serves about 8

CHAPTER 2

Yummy

Jamie loved the school lunches in elementary school. Every now and then he and Bobby wanted to carry their lunches, mostly just for show.

This is Bobby's first-grade picture.

Lunches

Stone Soup

Have your adult helper read this story to you.
Write down the list of ingredients as you hear them in the story.
When the story is completed, turn the page and read the list of ingredients,
then put the ingredients in a pot and cook them to make delicious soup!
There is one ingredient that *should not* be in the soup! Can you identify it?
Make sure you remove that ingredient before you serve the soup.

Once there was a tired traveler who had been walking a long way. He came to a village and knocked on the door of the first house he came to. A woman answered the door, and he said, "I am hungry and tired. Do you have anything I can eat?" She said, "No, I don't have anything myself!" She shut the door.

The traveler went on through the town and the same thing happened at each door. He began to think that if everyone had a little something, perhaps they could put it all in a pot and cook it, and then share it among themselves.

So to get things started, the traveler set up a pot at the edge of town, built a fire, put water in the pot, and said, "I'll make stone soup." He dropped a smooth, clean stone into the pot and began to stir.

A man stopped by. "What are you doing?" he asked.

"I'm making stone soup," the traveler responded. He tasted the water. "It's good, but it would be even better if it had a meaty ham bone in it!"

The man ran home and soon returned with a meaty ham bone.

Another curious villager stopped by and asked the same question. The traveler sent him home to find some carrots.

Another curious villager stopped by and the traveler sent him home to fetch some potatoes.

Another curious villager stopped by and the traveler sent him home to find some celery. He returned with celery *and* onions!

Another villager had a can of green beans. And yet another had a can of corn. Still another had a can of tomatoes. Another villager stopped by and was sent to bring back some salt and pepper!

Finally the traveler tasted the soup and declared that it was delicious. He removed the stone (that is what *does not belong* in the soup), and invited all of the villagers to share it.

The moral of the story is that when we share
what we have, we all benefit!

What you'll need to make Stone Soup

Medium pot with a lid

Liquid measuring cup

Vegetable peeler

Small, sharp knife

Medium, sharp knife

Cutting board

Measuring spoons

Dry measuring cup ($1/2$ cup)

Ladle

Soup bowls

1 meaty ham bone or slice of ham, minced

4 cups water

2 carrots, washed

1 medium baking potato or 2 small white potatoes, washed

2 stalks of celery, washed

1 small yellow onion, peeled

One 8.75-ounce can of cut green beans

One 8-ounce can of corn kernels

One 14$1/2$-ounce can of stewed or diced tomatoes

$1/2$ cup alphabet noodles, or macaroni noodles if you can't get the alphabet noodles

1 teaspoon salt and $1/4$ teaspoon pepper

What you'll do

1. Place the ham bone in the pot with the water. With an adult helper nearby, turn on the heat to medium and put the lid on the pot. Boil the ham bone for 20 minutes while you get the vegetables ready.

2. Take the vegetable peeler, and, with an adult helper, pare the carrots. Then, with an adult helper, slice the carrots with the small knife on the cutting board into little coins about $\frac{1}{2}$ inch thick. With an adult helper, use the vegetable peeler to pare the potato, and cut the potato into chunks with the medium knife on the cutting board.

3. Have an adult helper remove the ham bone and pick any meat from it. Put the meat back in the pot. Discard the bone. Do not put any fat in the soup. Add the carrots and potato.

4. Cut off the tips and the bottoms from the celery, leaving just the pretty green parts. Using the small knife and the cutting board, slice the celery into little C-shaped slices about $\frac{1}{4}$ inch thick. Add the celery to the soup.

5. Let an adult dice the onion for you using the medium knife and the cutting board. If you try to cut the onion, you will cry because of the strong scent that comes from the onion.

6. Drain the juice from the beans and the corn in the sink. An easy way to do this is to take the top from the can, hold your hand over the can, and pour out the water through your fingers. Add the beans and corn to the soup. Add the tomatoes, juice and all. Put the lid back on the pot.

7. Let your soup cook for 15 minutes over medium heat, then add the noodles. Cook 5 minutes if you are using alphabet noodles, and 10 minutes if you are using macaroni noodles. (When you remove the lid, steam will come pouring out, so be careful not to burn yourself.) Add the salt and pepper, stir with the ladle, and serve.

Makes about eight $\frac{3}{4}$-cup servings

Fried Egg Sandwiches

What you'll need

Measuring spoons

Small nonstick skillet

Small bowl

Wide spatula

Butter knife

Small plate

2 tablespoons olive oil

1 egg per person

Salt and pepper

About 1 tablespoon mayonnaise

2 slices of white bread per person

What you'll do

1. Put the olive oil in the skillet and tilt the pan so that the oil coats the bottom. Ask your adult helper to help you put the pan on the cooktop and turn on the heat to medium. Heat the oil for about 1 minute.

2. Crack the egg on the side of the counter. Break the egg into the small bowl by pushing gently into the crack with your thumbs and pulling the two sides of the shell apart. Throw out the shell. Pour the egg on top of the olive oil. If it begins to sizzle and curl immediately, the heat is too high, so turn it down a little.

It should just bubble gently in the hot oil. Sprinkle salt and just a little pepper on your egg.

3. Let the egg cook until the white edges are completely set, then get your adult helper to use the spatula to flip the egg to the other side. Flatten the egg with the spatula so that all of the yellow part comes out. Let that cook until the egg is completely done.

4. While the egg is cooking, spread the mayonnaise on one side of each bread slice and put one slice on the plate, mayonnaise side up. Let your adult helper gently lift the egg out of the olive oil and let a little of the oil drip from the egg. Put the egg on the bread on the plate. Top with the other slice. Serve right away.

Serves 1

Egg Salad
What you'll need

Medium, heavy
pot with a lid

Paper towels

Medium bowl

Potato masher

Dry measuring cup (¹⁄₃ cup,
for the mayonnaise)

Measuring
spoons

Rubber spatula

6 eggs

¹⁄₃ cup mayonnaise

¹⁄₂ teaspoon salt and
¹⁄₈ teaspoon pepper

1 tablespoon sweet
pickle relish

Crackers, or bread if you
want to make sandwiches

What you'll do

1. Place the eggs in the pot and cover them with water. Ask your adult helper to help you turn on the heat to medium-high and let the water come to a full, rolling boil. When it does, turn the heat off, cover the eggs with the lid, and let them sit for **45** minutes. (This will allow the eggs to finish cooking, and then will let the water cool down so that it will not burn you!)

2. Take the pot to the sink and drain the eggs. Gently tap the eggs on the side of the counter and peel away the shell. Rinse each egg under a little water, and lay on paper towels to drain.

3. Put the eggs into the bowl and mash them with a potato masher until they are in little shreds with no big chunks left. Do not let them get mushy, though.

4. Add the mayonnaise, salt and pepper, and pickle relish. Stir gently with the spatula until everything is mixed.

5. You can eat this on a plate with crackers, or use it in a sandwich.

Makes 1 cup, enough for
3 or 4 sandwiches

Cheese Quesadillas with Salsa

What you'll need

Cookie sheet

Small skillet

Dry measuring cup
(¹/₃ cup)

Measuring spoons

Wide spatula

Plate

One 10-inch flour tortilla

¹/₃ cup grated cheese—sharp Cheddar or Mexican blend

1 tablespoon canola oil

1 tablespoon sour cream

1 tablespoon mild salsa

What you'll do

1. Lay the tortilla flat on the cookie sheet. Sprinkle the cheese on one half of the tortilla. Try not to get it too close to the edge. Fold the tortilla in half over the cheese to make a half-moon.

2. Put the oil into the skillet. Ask your adult helper to help you place the skillet on the cooktop and turn the heat to medium. Heat the oil for about 1 minute.

3. With the spatula, gently transfer the tortilla to the pan, making sure none of the cheese falls out. Let the tortilla cook for about 2 minutes, until it is lightly brown. Take the spatula and gently lift the edge so you can check. When one side is brown, turn the tortilla over and cook the other side until it's brown and the cheese is all gooey.

4. Use the spatula to put the quesadilla on the plate. Top it with the sour cream and salsa. Enjoy!

Serves 1

Ambrosia Salad
What you'll need

Medium bowl

Dry measuring cup

Rubber spatula

One 15-ounce can of
mandarin oranges

One 8-ounce can of
crushed pineapple

1 cup miniature
marshmallows

$\frac{1}{2}$ cup sweetened
coconut

$\frac{1}{2}$ cup
sour cream

What you'll do

1. Drain the liquid from the oranges into the sink and put the oranges into the bowl.

2. Drain the liquid from the pineapple and put the pineapple into the bowl.

3. Add the marshmallows, coconut, and sour cream.

4. Mix gently with the spatula and serve.

Makes eight $^1/_2$-cup servings

Pineapple Cheese Spread

What you'll need

Small bowl

Rubber spatula

One 8-ounce block of cream cheese

One 8-ounce can of crushed pineapple

What you'll do

1. Unwrap the cream cheese and put it in the bowl. Let it sit out on the counter until it feels soft and gooey when you poke it with your clean finger, at least 1 hour. Wash your finger.

2. Drain the liquid from the pineapple into the sink. Put the pineapple into the bowl.

3. Mix well with the spatula. Use as a spread for a sandwich or stuff it into stalks of celery.

Makes about 2 cups

Olive Cheese Spread

What you'll need

Small bowl

Dry measuring cup

Cutting board

Medium, sharp knife

Rubber spatula

One 8-ounce block of cream cheese

1 cup green olives stuffed with pimientos

What you'll do

1. Unwrap the cream cheese and put it in the bowl. Let it sit out on the counter until it feels soft and gooey when you poke it with your clean finger, at least 1 hour. Wash your finger.

2. Ask your adult helper to help you with this—it's kind of tricky. Put the olives on the cutting board and chop them into very small pieces with the knife. The olives will want to roll around—that's the tricky part. But once you've chopped them first into big pieces, it's easier to chop them into little pieces. Put the olives in the bowl.

3. Mix well with the spatula. Use as a spread for a sandwich or stuff it into a stalk of celery.

Makes about 2 cups

Pigs in a Blanket
What you'll need

Parchment paper

Cookie sheet

Small,
sharp knife

Cutting board

Oven mitts or hot pads

Wide spatula

Big plate

1 can of refrigerated
crescent rolls (8 rolls)

4 hot dogs

Ketchup

Mustard

What you'll do

1. Turn on the oven to 375 degrees. Now, put the parchment paper on the cookie sheet.

2. Separate the dough into 8 triangles.

3. Cut each of the hot dogs in half crosswise. Place each hot-dog half on the wide end of a roll and roll it up. Space the hot-dog rolls evenly on the parchment—don't let them touch.

4. Ask your adult helper to help you put the cookie sheet in the oven and bake for about 13 minutes, until the rolls are nice and brown.

5. Have an adult, using oven mitts or hot pads, take the cookie sheet out of the oven. Transfer the pigs to the plate with the spatula. Let the pigs cool for a few minutes so that no one burns their fingers or mouth.

6. Serve with ketchup and mustard.

Makes 8 pigs

Applewiches
What you'll need

Medium,
sharp knife

Cutting board

Measuring
spoons

Butter knife

2 small plates

1 red or green
apple, washed

2 tablespoons
peanut butter

2 slices of mild
Cheddar cheese

What you'll do

1. Ask an adult helper to slice the apple into 4 circles.

2. Spread the tops of 2 apple slices with 1 tablespoon of peanut butter each.

3. Put a slice of cheese on top of the peanut butter.

4. Top with another slice of apple for the top of the sandwich. Put each sandwich on a plate and serve right away.

Makes 2 applewiches

Personal Pizza
What you'll need

Tray from the
toaster oven

Measuring
spoons

Butter knife

Oven mitt or hot pad

Wide spatula

Small plate

For each pizza

One-half of an
English muffin

1 tablespoon
pizza sauce

2 tablespoons grated
Cheddar or mozzarella
cheese

Toppings

4 slices of pepperoni, 1 teaspoon chopped green pepper (washed),
1 teaspoon chopped black olives, or other topping you like

What you'll do

1. Turn on the toaster oven to 375 degrees.

2. Put the English muffin on the tray, cut side up. Spread it with the pizza sauce. Top the sauce with the grated cheese. Top that with the pepperoni, green pepper, and black olives, or whatever toppings you like.

3. Put the tray in the toaster oven and bake until the cheese is bubbly, 6 to 8 minutes.

4. Use an oven mitt or hot pad to take the tray out of the toaster oven. With the spatula, put the pizza on the plate. Let it cool for about 1 minute, so that you don't burn the roof of your mouth.

Makes 1 pizza

CHAPTER 3

What's for

As a toddler,
Jamie ate a lot of
Vienna sausages.
I was afraid he
would choke.
But he didn't!

Dinner?

Meat Stew with Veggies
What you'll need

Dry measuring cup
(1/3 cup)

Measuring spoons

Gallon-size resealable plastic bag

Colander

Large skillet

Tongs

Slow cooker

Vegetable peeler

Medium, sharp knife

Cutting board

Liquid measuring cup

Wooden spoon

Ladle

4 soup bowls

1/3 cup all-purpose flour

2 1/2 teaspoons salt and 1/4 teaspoon pepper

1 pound lean stew beef, trimmed of all fat

2 tablespoons vegetable oil

1 package dry onion soup mix

3 carrots, washed

1 large baking potato, washed

2 stalks of celery, washed

2 1/4 cups water

1 tablespoon cornstarch

Cooked white rice

What you'll do

1. Put the flour, salt, and pepper in the plastic bag. Add the stew beef, close the bag tightly, and shake it up to coat all the pieces of meat with the flour mixture. Open the bag and, with the colander over the trash can, dump the meat into it. Shake the colander and let the extra flour fall through.

2. Heat the oil in the skillet over medium heat. (You should ask your adult helper to help because the hot grease pops out of the skillet.) When you can see ripples in the oil, put the meat into the skillet in one layer. Use the tongs to pick the pieces up and turn them over one by one when they're brown on the bottom. Cook them until they are brown all over. Turn off the heat and use the tongs to put the meat into the slow cooker. Sprinkle the soup mix on top of the beef.

3. Pare the carrots and the potato with the vegetable peeler. Cut each carrot into 5 or 6 pieces and let your adult helper cut the potato into chunks. Cut the celery into 1-inch pieces. Add all of the vegetables and 2 cups of the water to the slow cooker. Stir and cover.

4. Set the control to high and let the stew cook for 4 hours.

5. Set the control to low and let the stew cook for 3 hours more.

6. About 15 minutes before serving the stew, measure $\frac{1}{4}$ cup water. Stir in the cornstarch until there aren't any lumps. Add this to the stew and stir. Let the stew thicken for 15 minutes.

7. Put the rice into the soup bowls and ladle the stew on top.

Makes 4 servings

Chicken Pot Pie

What you'll need

Medium pot

Tongs

Cutting board

Medium, sharp knife

Liquid measuring cup

Measuring spoons

Small pot

Dry measuring cup ($^{1}/_{4}$ cup)

Whisk

9-inch glass pie plate

Oven mitts or hot pads

Scoop for serving

2 chicken breasts, with bone and skin

2 to 3 cups cold water

4 tablespoons butter

$^{1}/_{4}$ cup flour

1 cup whole milk

1 teaspoon salt and $^{1}/_{4}$ teaspoon pepper

Two 9-inch refrigerated foldable pie crusts

Two 15-ounce cans of mixed vegetables

What you'll do

1. Turn on the oven to 375 degrees.

2. Make sure your adult helper is nearby. Put the chicken and enough water to just cover it in the medium pot. Put the pot on the cooktop and turn on the heat to medium-high. When the water comes to a boil, cook for 25 minutes. Turn off the heat and let the chicken cool for 1 hour.

3. Using tongs, take the chicken out of the pot and put it on the cutting board. Pull the meat from the bones and chop it into medium-size pieces. Throw away the skin and bones and fat. Save 1 cup of the chicken broth to make your sauce.

4. Put the butter in the small pot over medium heat. When the butter is melted, add the flour and whisk it with the whisk until it is smooth. Slowly pour in the chicken stock and whisk until the sauce is thick. Add the milk and whisk until the sauce is bubbling. Whisk in the salt and pepper. Turn off the heat.

5. To assemble the pie: Unfold one of the pie crusts and press it into the bottom and sides of the pie plate. Spread the chicken over the bottom of the crust. Drain the vegetables (you can pour the water through your fingers into the sink). Spread the vegetables on top of the chicken. Pour the sauce over the chicken and vegetables.

6. Place the top crust over the chicken. Trim the edge if it is too long. Pinch the edges of the crust together. Take a knife and make 3 deep slits in the crust.

7. Bake the pie for 40 minutes, until the crust is brown and the filling is bubbling. Use oven mitts or hot pads to take it out of the oven. (You might have to ask your adult helper to do that for you.) Let the pie cool for 10 minutes before you take a big scoop.

Serves 6 to 8

Sausage Quiche
What you'll need

Medium skillet

Slotted kitchen spoon

Dry measuring cup
(1 cup)

Liquid
measuring cup

Small bowl

Whisk

Cookie sheet

Oven mitts or
hot pads

1 pound mild bulk
sausage

One 8-inch deep-
dish pie crust, in its
aluminum pie plate

2 cups grated sharp
Cheddar cheese

3 eggs

1 1/2 cups
half-and-half

What you'll do

1. Turn on the oven to 350 degrees. With an adult helper watching, sauté the sausage in the skillet over medium heat, breaking it up with the spoon as it cooks. Cook it until no pink remains, about 10 minutes. Using the spoon to lift it out of the skillet and let the fat drip back into the pan, spread the sausage in the bottom of the pie crust.

2. Sprinkle the cheese over the sausage. Break the eggs into the bowl (throw out the shells). Pour in the half-and-half and beat them together with a whisk. Pour the mixture over the cheese.

3. Put the quiche on the cookie sheet and have an adult help you put it in the oven. Bake the quiche for 35 to 40 minutes, until the center is not jiggly.

4. Using oven mitts or hot pads, take the quiche out of the oven. Let it sit for about 15 minutes before you cut it into wedges.

Makes 8 small wedges or 4 big ones

This is also good for breakfast or lunch.

Stuffed Shells
What you'll need

 Large pot

 Colander

 Measuring spoons

 Dry measuring cup (1 cup)

 Medium bowl

 Wooden spoon

 13 by 9-inch glass baking dish

 Rubber spatula

 Regular teaspoon

 Oven mitts or hot pads

 1 teaspoon salt

 20 large shell noodles

 1 pound small-curd cottage cheese

 1 cup grated Parmesan cheese

 Cooking spray

 2 cups spaghetti sauce, your favorite brand

 2 cups grated mozzarella cheese

What you'll do

1. With an adult helper nearby, turn on the oven to 350 degrees. Fill the pot three-fourths full of water and add the salt. Put it on the cooktop and turn on the heat to high.

2. When the water is boiling hard, add the noodles and cook until they are tender, 5 to 7 minutes. Have an adult drain the noodles for you in a colander in the sink. Let them cool for 20 minutes, until they are cool to the touch.

3. In the bowl, combine the cottage cheese and Parmesan, stirring well with the wooden spoon.

4. Spray the inside of the baking dish with the cooking spray. Pour a thin layer of sauce on the bottom of the dish and spread it out with the rubber spatula. With the teaspoon, place a heaping spoonful of the cheese mixture into each shell. Place the shells side by side on the sauce in the dish. If there is more cottage cheese left, use the teaspoon to drop the cheese onto the shells. Cover with the rest of the sauce, spreading it with the spatula. Sprinkle the mozzarella evenly on top of the sauce.

5. Put the baking dish in the oven. Bake it for about 25 minutes, until the mozzarella is bubbly and brown. Have an adult helper take it out of the oven with the oven mitts or hot pads, and let the shells cool for a few minutes before serving.

Serves 6 to 8

Pasta with Homemade Cheese Sauce

What you'll need

Large pot

Measuring spoons

Kitchen fork

Colander

Liquid measuring cup

Medium pot

Dry measuring cup (1 cup)

Wooden spoon

4 dinner plates

Ladle

1 teaspoon salt

One 8-ounce package angel-hair pasta

1 stick butter

1 cup half-and-half

1 cup grated Parmesan cheese

¼ teaspoon black pepper

What you'll do

1. Fill the large pot half full with water. Add the salt. With an adult helper nearby, put the pot on the stove and bring the water to a boil. Break the pasta in two and add it to the boiling water. Stir with the fork. Let the pasta cook for about 4 minutes, then lift one piece out with the fork and taste it. If it is tender, let your adult helper drain the pasta in the colander in the sink. Save a cup of the pasta water in the measuring cup.

2. In a medium pot, melt the butter over low heat. Add the half-and-half and the Parmesan cheese. Add the pepper. Stir with the wooden spoon just until the cheese is melted. Turn off the heat.

3. Put a cup of pasta on your plate. Ladle about one-fourth cup of sauce on top of the pasta and mix it in as you eat! If the sauce is too thick, you can add a little of the pasta water. You may want to add more sauce.

Serves 4

Pepperoni and Black Olive Pizza

What you'll need

Large cookie sheet
or pizza stone for
baking pizza

Liquid
measuring cup

Rubber spatula

Dry measuring cup
(1 cup)

Oven mitts or hot pads

Pizza cutter

1 premade pizza
crust

½ cup
pizza sauce

2 cups grated
mozzarella cheese

30 pieces of
pepperoni

One 5-ounce can
of sliced olives, liquid
drained into the sink

What you'll do

1. With an adult helper nearby, turn on the oven to 425 degrees.

2. Put the crust on the cookie sheet or pizza stone. Pour the pizza sauce on the crust, and use the rubber spatula to spread the sauce all around the crust. Don't put sauce on the rolled-up edges of the crust.

3. Sprinkle the mozzarella cheese all over the pizza, covering all of the sauce. Place the pepperoni and black olives evenly over the cheese.

4. Bake the pizza for about 18 minutes, until the cheese is bubbly. Ask an adult helper to take it out of the oven, using the oven mitts or hot pads. Let the pizza cool for a few minutes before you cut it into wedges with the pizza cutter.

Serves 6 to 8

Campfire Stew
What you'll need

Heavy-duty
aluminum foil

Dry measuring cup
($\frac{1}{2}$ cup)

Vegetable
peeler

Medium,
sharp knife

Cutting board

Cookie sheet

Oven mitts
or hot pads

$\frac{1}{2}$ cup
ground beef

1 carrot, washed

1 small white
potato, washed

Salt and pepper

What you'll do

1. Turn on the oven to 350 degrees. Tear off a piece of foil about 12 inches long. Crumble the beef evenly in the center of the foil.

2. Pare the carrot and the potato with the vegetable peeler. Ask your adult helper to chop the carrot into 1-inch pieces and cut the potato into eight pieces. Pile the carrots and potatoes on top of the ground beef. Give the whole thing 4 good shakes of salt and 1 shake of pepper.

3. Take the corners of the foil and bring them together. Twist the top and make sure there are *no holes* that the juices can escape from.

4. Put the foil package on the cookie sheet. Let your adult helper put it in the oven for you. Bake the stew for 1 hour.

5. Ask your adult helper to take the cookie sheet out of the oven with the oven mitts or hot pads. Let it sit on the counter for about 10 minutes before you unwrap the foil. Steam will come out, so be careful!

Serves 1

Spinach Salad
What you'll need

Small pot
with a lid

Paper towels

Medium skillet

Tongs

Large
salad bowl

Medium,
sharp knife

Cutting board

Dry measuring
cup (1 cup)

Liquid
measuring cup

Measuring
spoons

Medium jar
with a
tight-fitting lid

Large spoon

2 eggs

One 10-ounce
package of spinach,
washed and dried

4 slices
of bacon

Dressing

1 cup small
white mushrooms

6 cherry
tomatoes

1 cup
vegetable oil

1/4 cup red
wine vinegar

1/4 cup
lemon juice

1 teaspoon
salt and
1/2 teaspoon
pepper

1 tablespoon
sugar

1 teaspoon
dry mustard

1/4 teaspoon
minced garlic
(from a jar
is okay)

What you'll do

1. Cook the eggs: Put the two eggs in a small pot and cover with cold water. Bring the water to a boil, then put the lid on the pot and turn off the heat. Let the eggs sit for 45 minutes. Have your adult helper drain off the water so that you can then peel the eggs under cold running water. Dry on paper towels.

2. Fry the bacon in the skillet until it is crisp—let your adult helper help you because the bacon pops hot grease while it is cooking. Use the tongs to turn over the slices. Put the cooked bacon on a paper towel to drain, using the tongs. When it is cool, crumble it.

3. Place the spinach in the salad bowl and add the bacon. Let your adult helper help you slice the eggs into 8 wedges each. Cut the mushrooms into quarters. Cut the cherry tomatoes into halves. Add the eggs, mushrooms, and cherry tomatoes to the spinach.

4. Put all of the dressing ingredients into the jar. Cover tightly with the lid. Shake until the dressing is mixed.

5. Put about one-half of the dressing onto the spinach and then stir gently with a large spoon. Taste and see if you have enough dressing. If not, add a little more. (You can keep the rest in the refrigerator and use it on other salads.)

Serves about 8

Tuna Melts
What you'll need

Aluminum foil

Cookie sheet

Medium bowl

Medium,
sharp knife

Cutting board

Grater

Dry measuring cups
(1 cup and $1/4$ cup)

Wooden spoon

Oven mitts or hot pads

One 6-ounce can water-
packed tuna, drained

2 stalks of celery, washed

$1/8$ of a small onion

1 cup grated sharp
Cheddar cheese

$1/4$ cup mayonnaise

4 buns—hamburger,
hot dog, or hoagie rolls

1 cup crushed
potato chips

What you'll do

1. Turn on the oven to 350 degrees. Tear off four pieces of foil big enough to wrap around the buns you have picked. Put the pieces of foil on the cookie sheet.

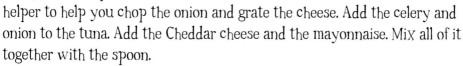

2. Put the tuna into the bowl. With an adult helper, slice the celery into thin pieces. Ask the adult helper to help you chop the onion and grate the cheese. Add the celery and onion to the tuna. Add the Cheddar cheese and the mayonnaise. Mix all of it together with the spoon.

3. Spoon about one-fourth of the tuna onto one-half of a bun. Repeat with the bottom halves of the other buns. On top of the tuna, sprinkle about $1/4$ cup of the potato chip crumbs. Put the lid on each bun. Put each bun on a piece of foil. Wrap them closed.

4. Have an adult put the tuna melts in the oven and bake them for 15 minutes, until the cheese is nice and runny. Ask the adult helper to use the oven mitts or hot pads to take the cookie sheet out of the oven.

Serves 4

Sloppy Joes
What you'll need

Medium,
sharp knife

Cutting board

Medium skillet

Wooden
spoon

Liquid
measuring cup

Measuring
spoons

1 small onion

1 pound
ground beef

2/3 cup ketchup

2 tablespoons
bottled mustard

4 hamburger buns

What you'll do

1. Have your adult helper chop the onion for you.

2. Put the hamburger and onion in the skillet. Put the skillet on the cooktop and turn on the heat to medium. Stir it all around with the spoon until every bit of pink in the hamburger has disappeared. Break up any large chunks of meat with the spoon. Let your adult helper help you drain the fat from the pan.

3. Add the ketchup and mustard and stir that around until it is all mixed in. Let this cook over the lowest heat for about 5 minutes, until it's good and mushy.

4. Put about one-fourth of the sloppy joe mixture onto each bun and enjoy!

Serves 4

Porcupine Balls

What you'll need

Medium
bowl

Dry measuring cups
(1 cup, $^1/_2$ cup, and
$^1/_4$ cup)

Measuring
spoons

2-quart
baking dish

Wooden spoon

Aluminum foil

Oven mitts
or hot pads

1 pound lean
ground beef

1 $^1/_4$ cups
uncooked
white rice

1 teaspoon
dried onion

1 teaspoon
seasoned salt

1 teaspoon
Italian seasoning

One 14-ounce can
of diced tomatoes
with juice

One
10 $^1/_2$-ounce
can of beef broth

What you'll do

1. Turn on the oven to 350 degrees.

2. Put the ground beef in the mixing bowl. Measure $\frac{1}{2}$ cup of the rice and put it in with the meat. Add the dried onion, seasoned salt, and Italian seasoning. Mix it all together with your clean hands. Roll it into 8 or 9 golfball-size balls of meat.

3. Put the rest of the rice in the bottom of the baking dish. Pour in the tomatoes and the beef broth and stir with the spoon. Put the meat balls on top. Cover the dish tightly with foil.

4. Bake for about 1 hour. Let an adult help you remove the dish from the oven with oven mitts or hot pads. When you remove the cover, steam will come out, so be careful! The rice in the meatballs will have puffed up all around the meat, and your meatballs will look like little porcupines!

Serves 4 to 6

Baked Potatoes

What you'll need

Paper towels

Fork

Cookie sheet

Oven mitts or hot pads

Dinner plates

Spoons for the garnishes

1 large, washed baking potato
per person

Vegetable oil

Grated Cheddar cheese

Sour cream

Butter

Bacon bits

What you'll do

1. Turn on the oven to 400 degrees. Wash the potatoes under running water. Dry them with paper towels. Take the fork and prick holes all over the potatoes. Rub the potatoes all over with a little oil. Then wash your hands. Put the potatoes on the cookie sheet so that they are not touching.

2. Bake the potatoes for 1 hour.

3. Ask an adult helper to take an oven mitt or hot pad and test the potatoes to see if they are done. Squeeze them gently, and if they feel tender, they are done. If they are not done, bake them for 15 minutes more.

4. Let the adult helper remove the potatoes from the oven with the oven mitts or hot pads. Put the potatoes on dinner plates and let each guest split theirs open with their dinner knife. Add grated cheese, sour cream, butter, and/or bacon bits—whichever they like.

Allow one potato per person

CHAPTER 4

I'm

I loved the school lunches. On Fridays we had vegetable soup, toast, and peanut butter balls (see recipe on page 104). That was my favorite day.

Bobby went to a four-year play school in Albany, Georgia, at Porterfield Memorial United Methodist Church.

Starving!

These are good snacks for after school, after supper, or on long Saturday afternoons.

Apples with Homemade Peanut Butter

What you'll need

Dry measuring cup
(1 cup)

Measuring
spoons

Food processor
(an adult must help
you with this!)

Small bowl

Cutting board

Small, sharp knife

Butter knife

2 cups shelled,
salted peanuts

2 tablespoons
cooking oil

½ teaspoon salt

Red or green
apple, washed

What you'll do

1. Let an adult help you put the peanuts in a food processor with the oil and the salt. Turn the machine on, let it run, and soon enough you'll have peanut butter! Let an adult help you scrape the peanut butter out of the food processor bowl (the blade is sharp, careful!) into a small bowl.

2. On the cutting board, with the sharp knife, cut the apple into thick slices. (You might want to ask for help with this, too.) Pick off the seeds and discard. Use the butter knife to spread peanut butter onto the apple slices.

Makes about 1 cup peanut butter

Cheese on a Log

What you'll need

Small bowl

Rubber spatula

Dry measuring cup
($^1/_4$ cup)

Small, sharp knife

Cutting board

Spoon

One 8-ounce
package grated
sharp Cheddar
cheese

One 8-ounce block of
cream cheese, softened

One 4-ounce
jar of pimientos,
with juice

$^1/_4$ cup mayonnaise

2 stalks of celery, washed

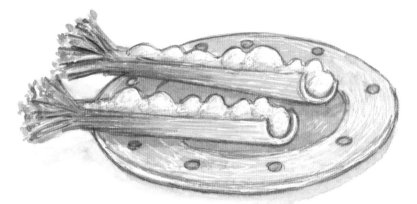

What you'll do

1. Put the Cheddar and cream cheese into the small bowl. Stir the two cheeses together with the spatula. Mix them well. Add the pimientos and mayonnaise and stir some more.

2. Let an adult help you cut the bottoms from the celery stalks. Stuff each stalk with about a tablespoon of the pimiento cheese. This spread is also very tasty on whole-wheat bread as a sandwich filling, or on a toasted English muffin.

Makes about 2 cups cheese spread

Honey Butter with Homemade Bread

What you'll need

Measuring
spoons

Small bowl

Rubber spatula

Liquid
measuring cup

Large bowl

Dry measuring
cup

Wooden spoon

Clean kitchen
towel

Wooden
cutting board

Two 9 by 5
by 3-inch loaf
pans

Oven mitts or
hot pads

Wire rack

Butter knife

1 stick
softened butter

1 tablespoon
honey

1 cup milk

3 tablespoons
sugar

1 tablespoon
salt

2 tablespoons
vegetable oil

1 cup
warm water

2 packages
dry yeast

5 cups all-purpose flour,
plus extra for kneading

Cooking spray

What you'll do

1. Put the butter and the honey in the small bowl. Let them sit out until the butter feels soft when you poke it (then wash your finger). Mix with the spatula. Cover and save for later.

2. Measure the milk in the liquid measuring cup. Put the cup in the microwave oven and microwave it for 40 seconds on high power, until it is slightly warm. Pour it into the large bowl. Add the sugar, salt, and vegetable oil and stir them well with the spatula. Measure 1 cup warm water from the tap. Put the yeast from the two packages into the water and stir with the spatula about 5 times. (This does not have to be mixed too well.) Let the mixture sit on the counter for about 10 minutes. Watch; it should bubble up pretty good!

3. Pour the yeast mixture on top of the milk and stir it well. Add the flour one cup at the time and mix well after you add each cup. Use a wooden spoon for this. You will probably need an adult to help you when the dough starts getting thick.

4. When all of the flour is mixed in, put a clean towel over the top of the bowl and put the bowl in a warm place. When you put the bowl aside, turn on the oven to 375 degrees. Let the dough rise for about 1 hour.

(continued on next page)

(continued from previous page)

5. Stir the dough down with the wooden spoon and then turn it out of the bowl onto a floured wooden cutting board. Knead the dough for about 2 minutes. This is a lot of fun—push down on the dough, squeeze it into a ball, then push down again. Keep on pushing and squeezing until the dough isn't sticky anymore. You will need to sprinkle the top of the dough with a little flour each time you turn it until it is no longer sticky.

6. Spray the loaf pans with cooking spray. Divide the dough in two equal pieces with your clean hands. Put half of the dough into each loaf pan and pat it down really well, so there are no airholes. Put a clean dish towel over the loaves and let them rise for 15 minutes. Remove the dish towel.

7. Bake the loaves for 35 to 40 minutes: the tops should be lightly browned and the bread should sound hollow when you tap on it.

8. Let an adult help you remove the pans from the oven with oven mitts or hot pads and place them on a wire rack to cool. In about 15 minutes, turn the bread out onto a cutting board and cut a thick slice. Spread it with that honey butter you saved.

Makes 2 small loaves of bread and 1 cup of honey butter. Leftover bread can be stored in a resealable plastic bag. Honey butter can be refrigerated. Let it sit at room temperature before using to make spreading easier.

S'Mores

Everybody knows this one, but maybe you didn't know
you can make it in the microwave oven! No need for a campfire!

What you'll need

Paper plate

2 graham
cracker squares

1 large
marshmallow

4 small squares
of a chocolate bar

What you'll do

Put one graham cracker square on the plate. Put the marshmallow on top of
the graham cracker square. Put the plate in the microwave. Microwave for
30 seconds on high power. The marshmallow will begin to melt. Let an adult
remove the plate and put a square of chocolate on the marshmallow. Put
another graham cracker square on top of the chocolate. Mash down on the
whole thing. Bite your s'more! But make sure it's not too hot before you bite.

Makes 1 s'more

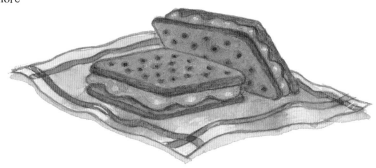

Homemade Pretzels
with Salt or Cinnamon

What you'll need

Liquid
measuring cup

Small pot

Dry measuring cups
(1 cup and $1/4$ cup)

Small bowl

2 large
bowls

Measuring
spoons

Wooden
spoon

Wooden
cutting board

Clean kitchen
towel

Cookie sheet

2 pastry
brushes

Oven mitts or
hot pads

Wire rack

1 package
dry yeast

6 tablespoons
($3/4$ stick) butter

1 egg

$1/4$ cup
sugar

1 teaspoon
salt

1 cup whole milk

5 cups all-purpose
flour, plus extra for
kneading and shaping

Cooking spray

Coarse salt

1/4 cup sugar mixed
with 1 teaspoon cinnamon

Mustard, if you are
making salted pretzels

What you'll do

1. Measure 1/2 cup warm water in the liquid measuring cup, then sprinkle the yeast on top. Stir it well, then let it sit for 10 minutes.

2. Put the butter in a small pot. Melt it over very low heat with your adult helper nearby. Measure out 1/4 cup and set that aside to cool. Set aside the pot for later.

3. Let an adult show you how to separate the egg white from the egg yolk. Keep the white in a small bowl. Put the egg yolk into the large bowl along with the sugar, salt, 1/4 cup melted butter, milk, and the yeast mixture. Stir with a wooden spoon until well blended. Start adding the flour, one cup at a time, stirring well after you add each cup.

4. After you have added all of the flour, turn the dough out onto a lightly floured wooden cutting board and knead it for about 5 minutes. Keep pushing down on the dough and squeezing it back into a ball until it isn't sticky anymore. Spray the inside of the other large bowl with cooking spray until it's all coated. Put the dough into the greased bowl and turn it so that all of the dough has been greased. Put a clean towel over the top of the bowl and let the dough rise for 1 hour in a warm place.

(continued on next page)

(continued from previous page)

5. Spray a cookie sheet all over with cooking spray. Turn on the oven to 425 degrees.

6. Divide the dough into 20 equal pieces with your clean hands. Roll each one into a rope. (This is my favorite part!) Have a plate of flour nearby in case your hands get sticky. Pat your hands, palms open, into the flour whenever you need to. Shape the ropes into pretzels (or anything you want, really!). Place them on the cookie sheet.

7. Take the egg white and add about a tablespoon of water to it. Mix this together really well with the pastry brush. Brush the tops of all of the pretzels with egg white. Sprinkle each one evenly with a little bit of coarse salt or lots of cinnamon sugar.

8. Bake the pretzels for 15 minutes, until they are light brown.

9. Have an adult help you take them out of the oven with oven mitts or hot pads. Put the cookie sheet on a wire rack. As soon as they're out, use a clean pastry brush to brush the tops of all of the pretzels with the melted butter you set aside before. The salted pretzels are really good with mustard!

Makes 18 to 20 pretzels

Ants on a Log
What you'll need

Small, sharp knife

Cutting board

Long, thin spatula or spoon

1 or 2 stalks of celery, washed

Peanut butter

Raisins

What you'll do

Let an adult help you cut a slice off the bottom of the celery. Scoop out about 1 tablespoon of peanut butter and use the spatula to press it into the hollow in the celery. When it's nice and even, set the raisins side by side into the peanut butter. Now you've got ants. Enjoy!

Makes 1 or 2 per person

Olive Pinwheels
What you'll need

Food processor
(an adult must help
you with this!)

Small bowl

Wooden
spoon

Cutting board

Butter knife

Sharp knife

Plastic container with a
tight-fitting lid

Paper towels

One 6-ounce can of
pitted black olives

One 5 $^3/_4$-ounce
can of pimiento-
stuffed green olives

One 8-ounce block of
cream cheese, softened

Four 10-inch flour
or whole-wheat
tortillas

What you'll do

1. Drain the liquid from the black olives and green olives into the sink. Put the olives into the bowl of a food processor and let an adult put on the lid and pulse about 5 times, until all of the olives are chopped up. Have an adult scrape the olives into the bowl for you, as the blade in the food processor is very sharp. Put the cream cheese in the bowl with the olives, and stir until the olives and cream cheese are all mixed up.

2. Take one tortilla and place it on a cutting board. Spread the tortilla with the olive mixture, leaving a border of about $1/4$ inch on the tortilla. Now roll up the tortilla very tightly and use a little dollop of cheese to "glue" the final edge together. Let an adult help you cut the tortilla rolls into pinwheels, about 1 inch thick. You should get about 9 or 10 pinwheels from each roll.

3. Place these in the plastic container. Put a slightly damp paper towel between the layers to keep the tortillas from drying out. Repeat with the rest of the tortillas and cheese.

Makes about 40 pinwheels

Peanut Butter Balls

What you'll need

Dry measuring cup
($^1/_2$ cup)

Liquid
measuring cup

Small bowl

Wooden spoon

Quart-size resealable
plastic freezer bag

Rolling pin

Waxed paper

Cookie tin

$^1/_2$ cup creamy
peanut butter

$^1/_2$ cup honey

$^1/_2$ cup nonfat instant
powdered milk

$^1/_2$ cup dry-roasted,
salted peanuts

What you'll do

1. Put the peanut butter, honey, and powdered milk into a bowl. Stir well.

2. Put the peanuts into the plastic bag. Roll your rolling pin over the bag to crush and crumble those nuts into tiny pieces. Put the crushed nuts onto the waxed paper.

3. Shape the peanut butter dough into little balls in the palm of your hand. Roll the peanut butter balls in the nuts.

4. Put a piece of waxed paper in the bottom of a cookie tin. Keep the peanut butter balls in the cookie tin.

Makes about 15 peanut butter balls

Gelatin Blocks

These will be sturdy enough to pick up and eat!
You can take them on car trips even without putting them into the fridge,
and they won't get runny! They are great for picnics, too.

What you'll need

Small glass bowl

Liquid
measuring cup

Metal stirring spoon

13 by 9-inch glass
baking dish

Butter knife or
cookie cutters

Four 3-ounce packages
of gelatin, any flavor
(strawberry, lemon,
lime, orange)

1 $1/2$ cups
boiling water

1 cup white
grape juice

What you'll do

1. Put the gelatin into a small glass bowl. Get an adult to help you heat the water to boiling in the microwave, about 2 minutes on high power. Pour the boiling water over the gelatin and then stir, stir, stir, until every bit of the gelatin has dissolved. Pour in the white grape juice. Pour the gelatin into the baking dish and refrigerate it until it is solid, about 3 hours.

2. To help the blocks come out of the dish better, fill the sink with about an inch of warm water. Dip the bottom of the dish into the water for about 30 seconds. Cut the gelatin into squares, rectangles, or use cookie cutters to cut them into fun shapes.

3. Store in a covered container in the refrigerator.

Makes about 20 to 24 blocks

Nuts and Bolts

Car trips, field trips, picnics, and parties—this is one great snack!

What you'll need

Dry measuring
cup (1 cup)

Very large
bowl

Liquid
measuring cup

Measuring
spoons

Spoon

Very large
roasting pan

Oven mitts or
hot pads

Resealable plastic
freezer bags

4 cups oven-
toasted rice
cereal squares

4 cups oven-
toasted wheat
cereal squares

4 cups oven-
toasted corn
cereal squares

2 cups
unsweetened
toasted oat cereal

2 cups small
pretzel sticks

1 cup nuts
of your choice
(I like pecans)

1 stick butter

1 tablespoon
seasoned salt

1 tablespoon
Worcestershire
sauce

What you'll do

1. Turn on the oven to 250 degrees. Put the cereals, pretzels, and nuts into a large mixing bowl. Have an adult help you melt the butter in the liquid measuring cup in the microwave for about 15 to 20 seconds at high power. Stir the seasoned salt and the Worcestershire sauce into the butter. Pour the butter over the cereals. Use your clean hands to mix everything together until all of the cereal is nice and coated with butter and sauce.

2. Spread out the cereal mix in a very large roasting pan. Put it into the oven and let it bake for about 1 hour, until it is crisp. Let an adult help you take the pan from the oven with oven mitts or hot pads.

3. When it is cool, store it in resealable plastic freezer bags.

Makes 17 cups

Doughnuts
What you'll need

Brown paper lunch
sack or resealable
plastic freezer bag

Paper towel

Big plate

Deep pot or electric
skillet for frying

Bottle cap

Tongs

Confectioners' sugar,
about 1 1/2 cups

1 quart
vegetable oil

1 can of refrigerator
biscuits (10 biscuits)

What you'll do

1. Put the sugar in the lunch sack and set it aside. Put a few sheets of paper towels on the plate and put the plate on the counter near the stove or electric skillet.

2. Put the vegetable oil in the pot or the electric skillet. It needs to be about 3 inches deep. Put the pot on the cooktop and turn on the heat to medium-high. If you're using an electric skillet, turn it on to 350 degrees.

3. Separate the biscuits. Take the bottle cap and punch a hole in the middle of each biscuit. Save the "holes" if you want to cook them, too.

4. Let an adult test the oil to see if it's hot enough—a drop of water sizzles in it when dropped in. Careful, hot grease is dangerous! Have an adult put the biscuit dough into the hot oil a few pieces at a time. Fry the biscuits until they are lightly brown on both sides, turning them with tongs. When you've fried all of the doughnuts, you can fry the "holes," too!

5. When they are done, have an adult remove them to the paper towel–lined plate. As soon as they have drained, put them immediately into the sugar. Close up the bag and shake, shake, shake until they are completely coated. Watch out! If the doughnuts are too hot, they will melt the plastic bag. Eat immediately!

Makes 10 doughnuts and 10 "holes"

Fruit Turnovers
What you'll need

Parchment paper

Cookie sheet

Cutting board

Sharp knife

Measuring spoons

Kitchen fork

Wide spatula

Liquid measuring cup

Wooden spoon

Oven mitts or hot pads

1 can of refrigerator biscuits (10 biscuits)

One 15-ounce can of fruit, like pears or peaches

$^1/_2$ cup white sugar, mixed with 1 teaspoon cinnamon

2 tablespoons ($^1/_4$ stick) butter, cut into 10 pieces

1 cup confectioners' sugar

$1^1/_2$ tablespoons milk or half-and-half

What you'll do

1. Turn on the oven to 375 degrees. Put a piece of parchment paper on the cookie sheet and another on the counter. Working on the countertop, pat each biscuit into a 4-inch circle. Drain the liquid from the fruit into the sink. Chop the fruit into little pieces.

2. Place about 1 tablespoon of the chopped fruit in the middle of each biscuit. Sprinkle with a little less than 1 teaspoon of the cinnamon-sugar mixture. Dot each with a piece of butter. Shape each biscuit into a semicircle by folding one side over to match the other side. Press with a fork all around the edge to seal. Using a spatula, transfer the semicircles to the cookie sheet.

3. Bake the pies for 10 to 12 minutes.

4. While the pies are baking, measure the confectioners' sugar in the glass measuring cup (you usually measure confectioners' sugar with a dry measuring cup, but we don't really want to have to wash two cups, do we?). Stir the milk into the sugar until it is very smooth. If the icing is too thick to stir, add just a drop or two more milk.

5. Let an adult help you take the pies from the oven using oven mitts or hot pads. While the pies are on the counter, dribble icing from the measuring cup all over the pies.

Makes 10 turnovers

Yogurt Pops

These are incredibly easy and a great, nutritious treat!
Perfect for a warm summer's day.

What you'll need

Small bowl

Liquid measuring cup

Spoon

Six 3-ounce
paper cups

8-inch square cake pan

Wooden pop sticks

One 8-ounce carton of
yogurt, any flavor

1/2 cup orange juice

1 tablespoon honey

What you'll do

1. Into the bowl, stir together the yogurt, orange juice, and honey. Pour the mixture into 3-ounce paper cups, filling each about three-quarters full. Put these in the cake pan to keep them steady. Put the pan in the freezer. Check on the yogurt cups in about an hour. When they have begun to freeze, stick a pop stick in the center of each one. When they are ready to eat, just peel the cup away.

2. You also can just freeze the yogurt in the cup with no stick and eat it with a spoon, like an Italian ice. Let it sit at room temperature for about 10 minutes before you start eating so it's not so hard.

Makes 6 pops

Frozen Bananas

What you'll need

Cookie sheet   Waxed paper   Dry measuring
                                           cup (1 cup)

Food processor (an adult
must help you with this!)

Paper plate   1-quart liquid   Measuring
                     measuring cup   spoons

Wooden spoon   Cutting board   Butter knife   Tongs

Plastic wrap

1 cup nuts—peanuts are
best, but you can also
use pecans or walnuts

2 cups
chocolate chips

1 tablespoon
milk or cream

4 bananas

Resealable plastic
freezer bag

What you'll do

1. Cover a cookie sheet with waxed paper.

2. Let an adult put the nuts in the food processor and pulse about 6 times to finely chop them. Put the chopped nuts on the paper plate.

3. Put the chocolate chips in the liquid measuring cup and add the milk or cream. Put the cup in the microwave oven for 40 seconds on high power. Remove and stir the chocolate chips. They should melt as you stir, but if you need to, you can microwave them for 10 seconds more and stir again. The chocolate should be thin and smooth.

4. Peel one banana and cut it in half crosswise. Using the tongs, dip each half into the chocolate and hold it over the cup to let all of the extra chocolate drip off. Roll the banana halves in the nuts. Set each chocolate-covered banana on the waxed paper and do the rest of the bananas.

5. When all are ready, cover with plastic wrap and freeze until firm. If you are not eating them immediately, store frozen bananas in a resealable plastic freezer bag.

Makes 8 frozen bananas

CHAPTER 5

Happy Birthday

This was Bobby's first birthday. You know, he still eats cake the same way today!

to ME!

These are recipes for cookies and cupcakes
you can take to school for your party.

Vanilla Cupcakes

Of all the many snacks served at birthday parties, these are the most popular.
You can certainly use a cake mix to prepare cupcakes, but these are safe
for any classmates who might be allergic to peanuts and peanut products.
However, you have to use butter, not margarine.

What you'll need

Dry measuring cup
(1 cup)

Large bowl

Electric mixer

Sifter

Waxed paper or
parchment paper

Measuring
spoons

Liquid
measuring cup

24 paper
cupcake liners

2 cupcake pans or
muffin tins

Oven mitts or
hot pads

Wire rack

1 1/2 sticks
butter, softened

2 cups white sugar

3 eggs

2 1/2 cups
cake flour

2 1/2 teaspoons
baking powder

1/8 teaspoon
salt

1 cup whole milk

1 teaspoon
vanilla extract

Sprinkles

Vanilla Icing

2 cups
confectioners' sugar

2 1/2 to 3
tablespoons milk

1 tablespoon
melted butter

1/2 teaspoon
vanilla extract

Food coloring,
optional

Chocolate Icing

1/2 stick
butter,
softened

3 tablespoons milk

3 tablespoons
cocoa powder

2 cups confectioners' sugar

1 teaspoon vanilla extract

(continued on next page)

What you'll do

1. Turn on the oven to 350 degrees.

2. To make the cupcakes, put the butter and white sugar into the large bowl. Have your adult helper beat the butter/sugar mixture with an electric mixer until the mixture is very smooth. Crack open the eggs, add them to the bowl, and beat well. (Throw out the shells.)

3. Put the sifter on a piece of waxed paper and put the flour, baking powder, and salt in it. Sift them together onto the paper. Add half of the flour mixture to the sugar mixture, along with half of the milk. Beat well, then add the rest of the flour mixture and milk. Add the vanilla and beat again.

4. Put 24 liners into the cupcake pans. Pour the batter into the liners, filling a little more than half full.

5. Bake the cupcakes for 18 minutes, or until lightly browned.

6. Get an adult to help you take the cupcakes from the oven using oven mitts or hot pads. Let the cupcakes cool on a wire rack for about 15 minutes before you ice them.

7. To make the vanilla icing, put the confectioners' sugar, milk, butter, and vanilla into the large bowl and have an adult beat well with the electric mixer until the mixture is very smooth. If the icing is too stiff, you can add a little more milk, a teaspoon at a time. You can add one drop of your favorite food color for fun. If you want a darker color, add two drops of food coloring.

8. To make the chocolate icing, put the butter, milk, cocoa powder, confectioners' sugar, and vanilla into the large bowl and have an adult beat well with the electric mixer until the mixture is very smooth. If the icing is too stiff, you can add a little more milk, a teaspoon at a time.

9. Spread a thin layer of icing on each cupcake. Top with your favorite sprinkles.

Makes 24 cupcakes

Peanut Butter Cookies

What you'll need

Parchment paper

Cookie sheet

Small bowl

Dry measuring cup (1 cup)

Electric mixer

Rubber spatula

Metal spatula

Wire rack

1 large egg

1 cup smooth peanut butter

1 cup sugar

30 Hershey's Kisses, unwrapped

What you'll do

1. Turn on the oven to 350 degrees. Put a piece of parchment paper on a cookie sheet.

2. Crack the egg into the small bowl. (Throw out the shell.) Add the peanut butter and sugar and beat with the electric mixer. Scrape down the sides of the bowl with the rubber spatula and mix again. Shape the dough into small balls and roll them in the palms of your clean hands. Put the cookies about 1 inch apart on the parchment paper.

3. Bake the cookies for 10 minutes.

4. Get an adult to help you remove the cookies from the oven using oven mitts or hot pads. Place the cookie sheet on the counter. Press a Hershey's Kiss in the middle of each cookie right away. Use the spatula to transfer the cookies to a wire rack to cool. The chocolate will melt a little bit, but when it hardens again, it'll be just like glue sticking the Hershey's Kiss to the cookie.

Makes about 30 cookies

Cookies on a Stick

What you'll need

2 cookie sheets

Parchment paper

Cutting board

Sharp knife

Pop sticks

Oven mitts
or hot pads

Metal spatula

Wire racks

Resealable
plastic bags

2 rolls of refrigerated
chocolate-chip cookie dough

One 14-ounce bag
of plain M&M's

What you'll do

1. Turn on the oven to 350 degrees.
Line the cookie sheets with parchment paper.

2. Take the wrapper off the cookie dough.
Put the dough on the cutting board and
slice it 1 inch thick. Insert a pop stick
into the side of the dough, about halfway
down, pushing the stick in at least 1 full inch.
Cover the top of each cookie with M&M's; press
them lightly into the dough. Put the cookies far
apart from each other so they will have plenty
of room to spread.

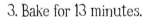

3. Bake for 13 minutes.

4. Have an adult help you remove them from the oven using oven mitts or hot
pads. Let them cool on the parchment for about 15 minutes, until the cookie
has hardened around the stick. Watch out: if you try to pick them up right
out of the oven, the stick will come out. After the cookies are cooled a little
bit, you can use the spatula to carefully remove the cookies from the pan and
put them on the wire racks to cool completely. Store carefully in resealable
plastic bags.

Makes about 18 cookies

Sheet Cake You Can Decorate

What you'll need

13 by 9-inch
cake pan

Oven mitts
or hot pads

Wire rack

14 by 10-inch piece of
cardboard, covered with
aluminum foil, or a cake board
from a cake-decorating store

Metal spatula

Sharp knife

Nonstick baking spray
with flour

1 recipe vanilla cake batter
from page 122

1 recipe vanilla or
chocolate icing from page 123

Sprinkles, M&M'S, or other candy, or
"scenes" from a cake-decorating store

What you'll do

1. Turn on the oven to 300 degrees. Spray the inside of a 13 by 9-inch cake pan with nonstick baking spray (the kind with flour in it).

2. Mix up the batter for the cake, but instead of putting it into cupcake pans, pour it into the pan. Smooth the top with a metal spatula.

3. Bake the cake for 25 to 30 minutes, until the sides pull away from the pan and the center appears set.

4. Have an adult help you remove the cakes from the oven using oven mitts or hot pads. Let it sit on a wire rack in the pan for about 10 minutes. An adult will also have to help you turn the cake out onto the piece of cardboard or cake board. Let the cake cool about 10 minutes more.

5. While the cake is cooling, make double the icing in the recipe you picked. That means multiply the amounts of all the ingredients by 2.

6. When the cake is cool, use the spatula to spread the icing all over it. Now, decorate the cake any way you want—with sprinkles, M&M'S, other candies, or with those little sets you can buy from a cake place—Western scenes, fishing scenes, ballet scenes, football scenes, or whatever. Decorating your own cake is tons more fun than buying one!

7. Cut the cake into rectangles to serve, with the birthday boy or girl getting to pick the first piece.

Serves 16 to 20, depending on size of pieces

CHAPTER 6

Cooking

Here I'm secure in the arms of my hero, my dad, at the River Bend Motel, in Albany, Georgia. My granddaddy built that motel, and I lived out there my first ten years of life. Church groups would come out 'cause we had it all—skating rink, restaurant, cabins. It was a great life.

for Mom and Dad

Nothing says "I love you" quite like a homemade meal for your mom and dad on their special day—birthdays or Mother's Day and Father's Day. You are going to need some help so that you have everything you need. Here are the things you need to do:

1. Make a card—you can do this with crayons and markers and plain white paper folded in half. You can write a poem, which is always nice, or just write a little paragraph about all the ways your mother or daddy helps you. Drawing a picture of yourself or your family makes the card extra special. Use lots of colors so it will be pretty.

2. Make a placemat for your tray. You will need two pieces of colored construction paper for this. Pick two colors that look pretty together, because you are going to "weave" one color through another—pink and green for your mother, for example, or brown and bright blue for your daddy. Take one piece of the construction paper and fold it in half the long way. Using a pair of safety scissors, cut about eight slits in your paper, an equal distance apart. Cut to within an inch of the edge. Unfold the paper so it lies flat. Now cut the second piece of construction paper into eight long, even strips. Weave the strips back and forth through the paper slits. When you are done, turn the placemat over and tape down the ends of the strips so they will stay put. To finish your project, buy some clear plastic adhesive with a peel-away back from a craft store. Peel the back away and put the adhesive on both sides of your mat. Cut the edges so that they are in line with the construction paper. You now have a placemat that you can use every time you serve a meal on a tray to your parent!

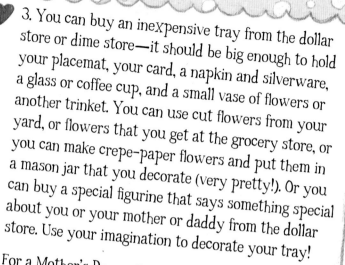

♥ 3. You can buy an inexpensive tray from the dollar store or dime store—it should be big enough to hold your placemat, your card, a napkin and silverware, a glass or coffee cup, and a small vase of flowers or another trinket. You can use cut flowers from your yard, or flowers that you get at the grocery store, or you can make crepe-paper flowers and put them in a mason jar that you decorate (very pretty!). Or you can buy a special figurine that says something special about you or your mother or daddy from the dollar store. Use your imagination to decorate your tray!

For a Mother's Day or Father's Day meal, you will need to get your tray ready on the Saturday before so you won't be rushed. Now you are ready to make the food!

Breakfast in a Cup

This is perfect for Mother's Day or Father's Day breakfast in bed.

What you'll need

Liquid measuring cup

Measuring spoons

Small nonstick pot with a lid

Dry measuring cup ($\frac{1}{2}$ cup)

Wooden spoon

Small nonstick skillet

Slotted kitchen spoon

Paper towel

Paper plate

Small bowl

Grits

Whisk

Rubber spatula

4 very large glass coffee cups with handles (try the dollar store for this)

1 teaspoon salt

$\frac{1}{2}$ cup quick-cooking grits

Sausage   Eggs

1 tablespoon butter

$\frac{1}{4}$ cup half-and-half

1 pound ground bulk country sausage

2 tablespoons butter

4 eggs

$\frac{1}{2}$ teaspoon salt
2 shakes of pepper

1 tablespoon sour cream

Grated cheese, for topping

Parsley leaves, for garnish (let your adult helper chop the parsley)

What you'll do

1. To make the grits: Have an adult who isn't celebrating their special day help you with this! Put 2 cups water and the salt in the saucepan. Put it on the cooktop over medium-high heat and let it come to a boil. Slowly stir in the grits—stir very well. Immediately reduce the heat to the lowest possible setting and add the butter. Let this cook for 4 minutes, then add the half-and-half and put the lid on the pot. Cook the grits up to 30 minutes, stirring occasionally. When they are done, turn off the heat and keep the lid on to keep them hot.

2. While the grits are cooking, have an adult help you cook the sausage. Crumble the sausage into the skillet with your clean fingers and then keep moving it around in the pan with the slotted spoon until every bit of pink disappears. This will take 10 to 12 minutes. Put a piece of paper towel on the paper plate. When the sausage is all cooked, use the slotted spoon to put it on the paper towel on the paper plate to drain.

3. Have an adult pour the grease from the skillet into the garbage (NOT down the drain!) and wash the skillet in hot, sudsy water. You can dry it.

4. You are ready to scramble the eggs. But you still need an adult to help you with these next steps. Put the butter in the skillet and place it over low heat to melt. When it is melted, break the eggs into the small bowl. (Throw out the shells.) Add the salt and pepper, 2 tablespoons water, and the sour cream to the eggs. Whisk this together until it is well blended. Turn the heat up to medium and when the butter sizzles, pour in the eggs. Let them cook on the bottom until they begin to "set" and look solid around the edges, then turn them three or four times, cutting large chunks apart with the edge of the spatula. As soon as the eggs are done, remove the skillet from the heat.

5. Assemble your breakfast in a cup: Spoon about one-fourth of the grits into each cup, top with about one-fourth of the sausage, and about one-fourth of the eggs. Top each cup with a generous sprinkling of cheese and a few leaves of parsley.

Serves 4

Hawaiian Beef Teriyaki Kebabs with Grilled Pineapple

And this is perfect for Mother's Day or Father's Day dinner.
Start this one the night before the big day!

What you'll need

Cutting board

Sharp knife

Liquid measuring cup

Measuring spoons

Gallon-size resealable plastic freezer bag

Big plate

Skewers

Pan big enough for skewers to fit into

Tongs

Meat platter

1 1/2 pounds sirloin steak

3/4 cup soy sauce

1 teaspoon minced ginger (available in jars)

1/2 teaspoon minced garlic (available in jars)

1 1/2 teaspoons brown sugar

One 20-ounce can of pineapple slices

What you'll do

1. Using the cutting board and sharp knife, get an adult to cut the steak into $\frac{1}{4}$-inch strips, cutting away all of the fat and gristle.

2. Put the soy sauce, ginger, garlic, brown sugar, and $\frac{1}{2}$ cup water in the plastic bag. Close the top and shake the ingredients together. Add the meat and seal it all up again. Turn it so that all the pieces are coated with marinade. Put the bag on a big plate and let it sit in the refrigerator overnight; all that good stuff needs some time to soak in.

3. About 30 minutes before you are ready to grill the meat, soak the skewers in a pan of water. Have your adult helper fire up the grill to high.

4. Thread the meat on the skewers longways, about two or three pieces of meat per skewer. (Careful, those skewers are pretty pointy.) Pour the marinade down the drain and throw out the bag. Drain the liquid from the pineapple slices into the sink.

5. Ask an adult to put the pineapple rings on the grill. Let them grill until they have dark grill marks and have begun to soften, about 10 minutes total. About halfway through, have the adult put the skewers on the grill. Turn the meat and pineapple with tongs. The meat has to grill for 4 to 5 minutes. Put the skewers on the platter and surround with the pineapple rings.

Serves 4

Magic Rice
What you'll need

Measuring
spoons

13 by 9-inch glass
baking dish

Dry measuring
cup

Kitchen fork

Aluminum foil

Oven mitts or
hot pads

One 10 $^1/_2$-ounce can
of beef broth

One 10 $^1/_2$-ounce can
of French onion soup

One 4-ounce can of button
mushrooms, undrained

2 tablespoons
melted butter

1 cup
white rice

$^1/_2$ teaspoon
black pepper

What you'll do

Turn on the oven to 350 degrees. Put the beef broth, French onion soup, mushrooms, and butter into the casserole dish. Add the rice and pepper and stir with a fork. Put the foil on the baking dish. Have an adult put the dish in the oven and let the rice cook for 1 hour. When it's ready, have the adult take it out using oven mitts or hot pads, and lift off the foil. Steam will come out, so be careful!

Serves 4

Broccoli with Magic Cheese Sauce

What you'll need

Cutting board

Sharp knife

Medium pot with a lid

Liquid measuring cup

Dry measuring cup

Measuring spoons

Medium glass bowl

Waxed paper

Spoon

Large bowl

1 bunch of broccoli, about 3 stems, washed

½ teaspoon salt

2 cups grated sharp Cheddar cheese

2 tablespoons sour cream

What you'll do

1. Let an adult cut the big, tough stems from the broccoli. Using your clean fingers, break the broccoli into bite-size trees and put them into the pot. Add 1 cup water and the salt. Put the pot on the cooktop and turn on the heat to medium-high. Bring the water to a boil, put the lid on the saucepan, reduce the heat to medium-low, and cook the broccoli for 8 minutes. Turn off the heat. Have an adult drain the water from the pot into the sink.

2. Put the cheese into the glass bowl. Dollop the sour cream on top. Cover this with a piece of waxed paper and put the bowl into the microwave oven. Microwave on high power for 45 seconds. Remove and stir. Be careful when you take off the paper—there might be steam! If all of the cheese hasn't melted, microwave for 15 seconds more. Don't overcook or the cheese will become stringy. Make this dish right before you serve it to Mom and Dad.

3. Put the broccoli into a serving bowl. Pour the cheese sauce over the broccoli.

Serves 4

Strawberry Delight
What you'll need

Large plastic bowl

Medium bowl

Electric mixer

Large glass bowl

Rubber spatula

Plastic wrap

1 large angel-food cake

One 8-ounce block of cream cheese, softened

One 14-ounce can of sweetened condensed milk, regular or fat-free

Two 10-ounce packages of frozen sweetened, halved strawberries, thawed

One 7-ounce can of whipped cream

1 pint ripe strawberries, rinsed, patted dry, and stems cut off

What you'll do

1. Tear the cake into bite-size pieces into the plastic bowl. Put the cream cheese and the sweetened condensed milk into the medium bowl and mix with the electric mixer until it is smooth.

2. Put about half of the cake pieces into the large glass bowl. Pour about half of the cream cheese mixture on top of the cake pieces and use the spatula to spread it evenly from one side of the bowl to the other. Open one package of strawberries and evenly pour the berries and juice over the cream-cheese mixture. Take the can of whipped cream and make a thin layer evenly over the strawberries—make sure you don't use it all because you need more for the top layer than you do for the bottom layer.

3. Repeat the layers—the other half of the cake pieces, the other half of the cream-cheese mixture, the other package of the strawberries and juice. Top off the whole thing with a thick layer of whipped cream. It will take the whole rest of the can. You can decorate the top with fresh strawberries, if you like.

4. Cover the top with plastic wrap and keep this in the refrigerator until after the meal is over. Then bring it to the table and everyone will *ooh* and *ahh* and think you are just the best cook ever.

Makes about 8 servings

CHAPTER 7

Treats

Here are Bobby and Jamie with Easter baskets that Aunt Peggy and Uncle George (Ort) created at their business, the Toy House.

Bobby and Jamie put gumballs on a plastic tree before Christmas. I made a gumball tree for Jack this year! Look at the cake on the counter—I was always cooking!

for the Holidays

Give your friends a taste of the season.

Halloween
Goober Haystacks

What you'll need

Dry measuring
cup

Measuring
spoons

Medium
glass bowl

Large spoon

Teaspoon

Waxed paper

1 cup butterscotch
morsels

1 tablespoon creamy
peanut butter

1 cup dry-roasted
peanuts

1 cup canned chow
mein noodles

Resealable plastic bags
or a plastic storage
container with a tight-
fitting lid

What you'll do

1. Put the butterscotch morsels and peanut butter into the mixing bowl. Microwave on high power for 1 minute, remove the bowl, and stir. The butterscotch morsels should melt as you stir, but if they don't, don't worry! Just put them back in the microwave oven for 15 seconds more and then stir again.

2. When the butterscotch is completely melted and smooth, stir in the peanuts and the chow mein noodles. This will be stiff and you may need an adult to help you. Use a teaspoon to scoop out a little of the mixture and mound it onto the waxed paper. These should look like haystacks.

3. Let them stand at room temperature until they are set. This will take 45 minutes to 1 hour. Store in resealable plastic bags or a plastic storage container with a tight-fitting lid.

Makes 20 to 24 small haystacks

Thanksgiving
Pumpkin Muffins

Pack these in your lunchbox!

What you'll need

2 cupcake pans or muffin tins

Cupcake liners

2 medium bowls

Dry measuring cups (1/4 cup, 1/2 cup, 1 cup)

Measuring spoons

Liquid measuring cup

Wooden spoon

Ladle

Oven mitts or hot pads

Wire racks

Butter knife

Nonstick baking spray with flour

2 cups all-purpose flour

1 teaspoon baking soda

1/2 teaspoon salt

1 teaspoon cinnamon

1/4 teaspoon allspice

3/4 cup light brown sugar

3 tablespoons molasses

1/4 cup canola oil

2 large eggs

One 15-ounce can of pureed pumpkin

1 teaspoon vanilla extract

3/4 cup buttermilk

148

What you'll do

1. Turn on the oven to 400 degrees. Spray 15 muffin cups with baking spray or place cupcake liners in muffin pans.

2. In a medium bowl, whisk together the flour, baking soda, salt, cinnamon, and allspice. In another bowl, whisk together the brown sugar, molasses, oil, eggs, pumpkin, vanilla, and buttermilk.

3. Add the liquid ingredients to the dry ingredients and stir together just until combined. Don't overmix! Muffin batter should be lumpy.

4. Ladle the batter evenly into the muffin cups, filling them about three-fourths full. Tap the pans on the counter to make sure you get out the air bubbles. Bake for 20 minutes.

5. Have an adult help you take the pans out of the oven using oven mitts or hot pads. Put the pans on a wire rack to cool for 5 minutes. Run a butter knife around the muffins so that you can loosen them from the pans. Let them cool completely on the wire rack.

Makes 15 muffins

Christmas Chocolate-Covered Pretzels with Sprinkles

These make great gifts! Start these the day before you want to eat 'em or give 'em to your friends and family!

What you'll need

2 medium shallow bowls

Rubber spatula

Waxed paper

Plastic gift bags

Curly ribbon

Gift cards

Tape

One 12-ounce package of milk-chocolate morsels

One 12-ounce package of white chocolate morsels

24 large pretzel rods

1 small container of holiday sprinkles

What you'll do

1. Put the milk-chocolate morsels in one bowl. Put the white-chocolate chips in the other bowl. Put one bowl in the microwave and microwave on high power for 1 minute. Remove and stir with a spatula; the morsels should melt while you are stirring, but if they don't, you can microwave the bowl for 15 seconds more, then stir again.

2. Put the other bowl in the microwave and microwave on high power for 1 minute. Wash and dry the spatula, then stir these morsels. Again, if the morsels don't melt, microwave for 15 seconds.

3. Dip one pretzel rod into the milk chocolate, about halfway up the rod. Twist to let the excess chocolate drip off. Hold the rod over a piece of waxed paper and sprinkle with sprinkles on all sides of the chocolate—using the tips of your clean fingers to sprinkle works best. Place the pretzel on another piece of waxed paper to dry. Coat another pretzel rod with white chocolate and sprinkles. Keep going until you have coated all of the pretzels, half with milk chocolate and half with white chocolate. It will take the pretzels about 24 hours to dry completely.

4. Put two to four pretzels in each of your gift bags, chocolate side down. Tie the tops with curly ribbon. Make little cards and tape the back of the package.

Makes 24 large pretzels

Valentine's Day
Crispy Rice Hearts

This makes individual hearts. You can also make giant hearts by
pressing half of the cereal-marshmallow mixture into two heart-shaped cake pans
that you sprayed first with cooking spray. Everyone gets a piece of the heart.
It's a little messy to cut, but sure looks neat on the table.

What you'll need

Large pot

Large spoon

Rubber spatula or
waxed paper

Cookie sheet

Heart-shaped
cookie cutter

4 tablespoons
(½ stick) butter

One 10-ounce
package of regular
marshmallows

5 cups crisped rice
cereal, like Rice
Krispies

Cooking spray

Red or white
icing in tubes,
if you like

Plastic container
with a
tight-fitting lid

What you'll do

1. Put the butter in the pot with the marshmallows. Have an adult heat them on the cooktop over low heat. Stir until they are completely melted.

2. Have an adult remove the pot from the heat. Add the cereal and stir until the cereal is coated with the marshmallow mixture.

3. Spray cooking spray on the spatula or on a piece of waxed paper. Spray the cookie sheet. Use the spatula or the waxed paper to spread the cereal mixture on the cookie sheet and press it about $1/4$ inch thick and as even as you can get it.

4. Let it harden for 30 minutes. Use a heart-shaped cookie cutter to cut hearts. You can decorate these with red or white icing, if you like.

5. Store in a plastic container with a tight-fitting lid for no more than 2 days.

Makes about 10 to 12 hearts, depending on size of the cutter

Easter
Dyed Eggs
What you'll need

Large pot with a lid

Paper towels

Crayons or markers

Food coloring or
an egg-coloring kit

Glass bowls or
plastic deli take-
out containers

Measuring
spoons

2 cardboard rolls from
paper towels or a wire rack
and newspaper sheets

Stickers, ribbon,
sequins, etc.,
if you like

Glue, if you're using
sequins or ribbon

1 dozen eggs

Vinegar

What you'll do

1. Put the eggs in the pot. Cover them completely with water. Turn on the heat to medium-high and let the water come to a full, rolling boil. When it does, turn the heat off, put the lid on, and don't take it off again for 20 minutes.

2. Have an adult take the pot to the sink and drain off the hot water before you rinse the eggs in cold water until they are cold. Put them on paper towels to dry completely before you begin to dye them.

3. You can now use crayons to color the eggs—the dye will "take" on the parts that you leave white. Or you can dye the eggs first and then use markers to color on the eggs.

4. Here is how you dye the eggs: Put about 4 inches of water in several glass bowls. (The dye will ruin your plastic dishes, but if you save plastic containers from your local deli, those work great.) Add a few drops of food coloring and 1 tablespoon of vinegar to each dish. Make as many colors as you like. (Or you can buy an egg-coloring kit and use those colors.) Put a few eggs into each bowl. The longer an egg sits in the water, the deeper the color it will be, so leave it for a shorter time if you want pastels (light colors).

5. Have an adult cut the paper towel rolls into twelve 2-inch pieces. Stand an egg in each piece so it can dry. Or dry the eggs on wire racks, placed over a layer of newspaper and paper towels. (The dye will stain your countertops if you don't protect them!)

6. When the eggs are dry, you can glue on any decorations you like—sequins, ribbon, etc.—or use stickers. Make sure you don't press down too hard, or you will crack the egg shells. But I think the prettiest eggs, however, are just plain!

7. Boiled eggs must be kept in the refrigerator, but are okay to eat even if they've been at room temperature for 2 hours if you want to use them as a centerpiece or in an egg hunt. After 2 hours, eggs should be eaten or returned to the refrigerator.

Makes 12 eggs

CHAPTER 8

Special

Bobby with Jamie, holding cousin Corrie Hiers in her Easter bonnet in Albany, Georgia

Drinks for All Year

Lemonade

Kids in Savannah still have lemonade stands on hot days.
Selling lemonade is a great way to meet your neighbors!

What you'll need

Dry measuring cup
(1 cup)

Liquid
measuring cup

1-gallon
container

Large spoon

Cutting board

Sharp knife

Small bowl

Strainer

Tall glasses

2 cups sugar

1 cup hot water,
from the tap

13 lemons

Ice cubes

Mint sprigs, for garnish

What you'll do

1. Measure the sugar and the hot water into the gallon container. Stir until the sugar has dissolved and disappeared!

2. Have an adult help you cut 12 of the lemons in half. Squeeze the lemon juice into the bowl. You will get tired doing this, but keep going until the job is done! Use the strainer to fish the seeds out of the juice. You want to keep all of the lemon pulp in the juice because it makes the lemonade taste better. You can throw out the empty lemon halves.

3. Add the lemon juice to the sugar water. Fill the container up with cold water. Let an adult help you slice the thirteenth lemon into thin slices. Take out all of the seeds and put the lemon slices into the gallon container. Stir it up well. If you won't be serving it right away, put it in the refrigerator.

4. To serve, put a few ice cubes into each glass. Pour the lemonade over the ice. Don't forget to put a mint spring in each glass.

Makes 1 gallon, about twenty 6-ounce servings

Yogurt Fruit Smoothies

What you'll need

Blender

Measuring spoons

Liquid measuring cup

3 drinking glasses

Any soft fruit—1 banana, one 15-ounce can of canned pears, one 15-ounce can of canned peaches, $\frac{1}{2}$ cup blueberries (washed), or $\frac{1}{2}$ cup strawberries (washed; canned fruit does not have to be drained; you want to keep all of the yummy flavor)

One 8-ounce carton of vanilla yogurt

1 tablespoon honey

2 cups ice cubes

What you'll do

1. Put the fruit, yogurt, honey, and ice in the blender. Put the lid on. Blend it until it is smooth. Be prepared for a loud noise!

2. Pour it into glasses.

Makes three 6-ounce servings

Vanilla or Chocolate Shake

What you'll need

Dry measuring cups
(1/4 cup, 1 cup)

Measuring
spoons

Liquid
measuring cup

Blender

4 tall glasses

3 cups vanilla
ice cream

2 teaspoons
vanilla extract

1/4 cup sugar

1 cup milk

1/4 cup
chocolate syrup
(for chocolate shake)

What you'll do

1. Measure all of the ingredients into the blender. Put on the lid. Turn it on and blend until the shake is smooth.

2. Pour into 4 glasses.

Makes four 8-ounce shakes

Lime Sherbet Punch

This makes a lot, so you want to do it for a party—a birthday or St. Patrick's Day or whenever you're in the mood for a green drink!

What you'll need

2-gallon punch bowl

Large spoon

Ladle

Paper cups or plastic glasses

½ gallon lime sherbet

6-ounce can of frozen limeade

2-liter bottle lemon-lime soda

What you'll do

1. Put the lime sherbet into the punch bowl. Add the frozen limeade. Pour the soda over them so that they will begin to melt. Leave the punch alone for about 15 minutes, then come back to it and stir until it is nice and creamy.

2. Ladle the punch into glasses to serve.

Makes about sixteen 6-ounce servings

Grape, Orange, or Root Beer Floats

These are the easiest, best drinks in the world!

What you'll need

Ice-cream scoop

Tall glass

Vanilla ice cream

Grape, orange, or
root beer soda

What you'll do

Put two medium scoops of ice cream in the glass. Pour in the soda almost to the top of the glass. No need to stir! The ice cream will get icy and the soda will get creamy.... It's just great!

Makes 1 float

Hot Chocolate

What you'll need

Dry measuring cup
(1/2 cup)   Medium pot   Whisk   Liquid measuring cup

Ladle   6 mugs   1/2 cup sugar

1/2 cup cocoa powder   1 quart whole milk (not low-fat)   One 7-ounce can of whipped cream   Mini marshmallows

What you'll do

1. Put the sugar and cocoa into the pot and whisk together. Pour in the milk and whisk again. Put the pot on the cooktop and turn on the heat to very low. Heat until it is hot but not boiling—this takes 8 to 10 minutes. Stir occasionally with the whisk, making sure that you mix in all of the cocoa.

2. Ladle into mugs and top each one with a squirt of whipped cream or a handful of mini marshmallows, or both!

Makes six 6-ounce servings

CHAPTER 9

Don't Eat Fun Arts

Jamie and Bobby get a bear hug in Columbus, Georgia.

These!
and Crafts

Some of our favorite recipes aren't meant to be eaten!
Here are things you can "cook up" in the kitchen to entertain
yourself or to give as gifts.

Play Clay

When playing with play clay, it's fun to use rolling pins,
cookie cutters, and plastic knives and forks for decorating your creations.
Make several batches in different colors.

What you'll need

Dry measuring cups
($^1/_4$ cup and 1 cup)

Measuring
spoons

Medium pot

Liquid
measuring cup

Large spoon

Resealable plastic
bag or plastic cover
with a lid

1 cup all-purpose
flour

$^1/_4$ cup salt

2 tablespoons
cream of tartar

2 to 3 drops
food coloring

1 tablespoon
vegetable oil

What you'll do

1. Measure the flour, salt, and cream of tartar into the pot and stir together with the spoon. Combine food coloring and oil with 1 cup water in the measuring cup and stir. (The more drops of food coloring you use, the deeper the color of the play clay. Start with 2 drops and see if you like the color. Add one drop at a time until you get the color you like!) Add it to the dry mixture. Put the pot on the cooktop and turn on the heat to medium. Cook over medium heat for 3 to 5 minutes. It will get hot, so let an adult stir it for you. It will start "globbing" together, and when it forms a ball in the middle of the pot, it's done.

2. Have an adult help you turn the glob out onto the counter. Let it cool for 10 minutes before you touch it. Careful, it is HOT! Knead it until the color is all mixed in and the dough is workable. Store in a resealable plastic bag or plastic container with lid.

Makes about 2 cups of play clay. Will last a long time!

Salt Dough

You can use this to make just about any creation.
You bake the dough and then you can keep your creation forever!

What you'll need

Dry measuring cup
(1 cup)

Medium bowl

Liquid
measuring cup

Rolling pin

Cookie cutters

Drinking straw

Toothpicks

Cookie sheet

Oven mitts
or hot pads

Sandpaper

Acrylic paint

Paintbrush

Clear plastic
spray sealer

2 cups all-
purpose flour

1 cup salt

1/2 teaspoon alum
(you can get this at
the health food store)

What you'll do

1. Put the flour, salt, and alum into the bowl, add $^3/_4$ cup water, and mix with your clean hands. Form the shapes you want—you can roll the dough flat (no more than $^1/_4$ inch thick) and use cookie cutters to make ornaments, or whatever you're in the mood to make. Choose small cookie cutters—2-inch cutters work well—as your ornaments will be heavy after they've baked.

2. If you are making ornaments, think about how you will hang them—you may want to make a hole in the top with a straw so that you have a place to put a piece of yarn through for hanging. You may also want to personalize your ornament by putting your name and the date on the back of the ornament, writing with a toothpick like you do with a stick on the beach.

3. Turn on the oven to 250 degrees. Put your creations on the cookie sheet. Bake them for about 2 hours. Have an adult help you take them out of the oven using oven mitts or hot pads.

4. When the ornaments are cool, you can rub any rough edges smooth with a small piece of sandpaper.

5. Paint them with acrylic paint, available at a craft store. Allow the paint to dry. Paint the other side. Allow the paint to dry. Spray with clear plastic spray sealer, also available in the craft store. You can display your creations, or store them in small tins if you want to keep them from year to year.

How many this makes depends on the designer! If you are rolling out the dough and using cookie cutters, it can make up to 2 dozen $2^1/_2$-inch ornaments.

Giant Bubbles

Do this on a rainy day when there's nothing to do.
The damp air makes the bubbles bigger and last longer before they pop.

What you'll need

1 large wire
coat hanger

Liquid
measuring cup

Large, flat pan, big
enough for the coat
hanger circle to fit into

Whisk

½ cup
dishwashing liquid

4 ½ cups
cold water

What you'll do

1. Get an adult to bend the coat hanger into a circle for you, making sure there aren't any rough ends that could scratch you.

2. Mix the dishwashing liquid and the water in the large flat pan. Whisk the two together.

3. When the rain stops, go outside with your supplies. Dip the coat hanger into the bubble solution and lift it straight up, then wave it through the air. Giant bubbles should appear!

4. If you have leftovers, keep them in a jar and use them again. They won't go bad!

Makes 5 cups, enough for lots and lots of bubbles!

Index